Linking AutoCAD To 3D Studio R2 *for Architecture*

Michele Bousquet
John McIver
Daniel Douglas

Autodesk.
Press

 An International Thomson Publishing Company

Albany • Bonn • Boston • Cincinnati • Detroit • London • Madrid
Melbourne • Mexico City • New York • Pacific Grove • Paris • San Francisco
Singapore • Tokyo • Toronto • Washington

Trademarks

AutoCAD, AME, 3D Studio, and the AutoCAD® logo are registered trademarks of Autodesk, Inc. AutoVision is a trademark of Autodesk, Inc. Windows is a trademark of the Microsoft Corporation. All other product names are acknowledged as trademarks of their respective owners.

COPYRIGHT © 1996
Delmar Publishers Inc.
Autodesk Press imprint
an International Thomson Publishing Company
For more information, contact:

The ITP logo is a trademark under license.
Printed in the United States of America

Autodesk Press
3 Columbia Circle, Box 15-015
Albany, New York USA 12212-5015

International Thomson Editores
Campos Eliseos 385, Piso 7
Colonia Polanco
11560 Mexico D. F. Mexico

International Thomson Publishing Europe
Berkshire House 168-173
High Holborn
London, WC1V 7AA
United Kingdom

International Thomson Publishing GmbH
Konigswinterer Strasse 418
53227 Bonn Germany

Thomas Nelson Australia
102 Dodds Street
South Melbourne, Victoria 3205
Australia

International Thomson Publishing France
Tour Maine-Montparnasse
33, Avenue du Maine
75755 Paris Cedex 15, France

Nelson Canada
1120 Birchmont Road
Scarborough, Ontario
Canada, M1K 5G4

International Thomson Publishing--Japan
Hirakawacho Kyowa Building, 3F
2-2-1 Hirakawa-cho Chiyoda-ku
Tokyo 102 Japan

International Thomson Publishing Southern Africa
Building 18, Constantia Park
240 Old Pretoria Road
P.O. Box 2459
Halfway House, 1685 South Africa

International Thomson Publishing Asia
221 Henderson Road
#05-10 Henderson Building
Singapore 0315

1 2 3 4 5 6 7 8 9 10 XXX 01 00 99 98 97 96

Library of Congress Cataloging-in-Publication Data

Bousquet, Michele, 1962–
    Linking AutoCAD to 3D studio r2 for architecture/Michele
Bousquet, John McIver, Daniel Douglas.
        p. cm.
    Includes index.
    ISBN 0-8273-8081-X
    1. Architectural drawings—Data processing. 2. Computer-aided design. 3. Computer animation. 4. AutoCAD (Computer file) 5. 3D studio   I. McIver, John. II. Douglas, Daniel. III. Title.
NA2728.B68   1996   96–2519
720′.28′402855369—dc20   CIP

TABLE OF CONTENTS

Chapter 3   AutoCAD Plans for 3D Studio

Chapter 4   3D Drawing in AutoCAD

Chapter 5   3D Studio Basics

Chapter 6   3D Studio Animation

Chapter 7   Visualization Techniques

INTRODUCTION

AutoCAD is the most popular technical drawing software in the world. Many thousands of architects, engineers, designers, and drafters have discovered the value of using AutoCAD as a drawing and design tool to simplify and speed up their work.

When AutoCAD was first released, it was capable of producing only 2D drawings much like those that were drawn manually. In recent years, AutoCAD has evolved to include commands for drawing in 3D. Even with the most sophisticated tools at hand, the architect still has to contend with a fundamental challenge with the drawings—often the design must be shown to and understood by people (clients) who can't read technical drawings.

With AutoCAD's 3D features, architects can use the drawing to present the design with pictures that simulate the final product. In order to do this, you need to understand what 3D drawing is, how it works in AutoCAD, and how you can use an AutoCAD model in 3D Studio to create your own renderings and animation for presentations.

Who Should Use This Book

This book is designed for those who are familiar with AutoCAD's 2D commands and are ready to make the leap to 3D. Using AutoCAD for 3D drawing requires an approach rather different from 2D drawing. For those who have been using AutoCAD in 2D for a substantial length of time, you may even have to learn a few new tricks to move successfully to 3D.

This book gives you the fundamentals of 3D modeling and animation, and provides you with all the knowledge you need to start working on your own projects in 3D and within 3D Studio. We hope you use this book to the best of your ability, then move on to fine-tune your approach to suit your projects.

Best of luck to you.
Michele Bousquet

ABOUT THE AUTHORS

Michele Bousquet has worked with 3D Studio since Release 1 and AutoCAD since 1991. She has co-authored eight books on the software. Michele splits her time between the United States and Australia, working as an animator, teacher, and writer. She is currently producing a series of videotapes on 3D Studio.

John McIver has been using AutoCAD since 1985. He started exploring 3D modeling and rendering in 1990 with Pixar's RenderMan, then moved on to 3D Studio starting with Release 1. John currently works as a freelance AutoCAD modeler based in Melbourne, Australia.

Daniel Douglas is a freelance computer animator specializing in architectural and engineering visualization. He has been using AutoCAD for 3D modeling since beginning his architectural education in 1990, and has two years' experience with 3D Studio. In addition to freelance work, Daniel teaches architectural modeling and rendering to designers in the Boston area.

HOW TO REACH US

To access Autodesk Press on the World Wide Web, point your browser to:

http://www.autodeskpress.com

Autodesk Press is an imprint of the International Thomson Publishing organization, http://www.thomson.com.

CHAPTER

1

FROM 2D TO 3D

A fact of life for the architect is that without clients there is no work. In seeking new clients, the architect looks for more interesting and attractive ways to present drawings.

An architect has the added challenge of communicating visual design concepts using very technical drawings. An architect's tools are technical drawings, yet most people cannot interpret them and thus cannot visualize the design clearly. The architect must portray the design in such a way that the client both understands it and finds it desirable.

In recent years an architect or drafter has been able to use AutoCAD to make the design process easier and quicker. Nowadays an AutoCAD drawing can be made in three dimensions, which makes it possible to present a design in a more understandable format.

VISUALIZATION

Visualization is the art of making pictures of a design before it has actually been built. With visualization, non-technical persons can see and understand a design much more easily.

In architecture, visualization has been around for a long time in the form of artists' renderings and scale models. The architect hires an artist adept at reading technical drawings, and the artist produces a color picture or scale model of the finished building. This type of visualization has been very useful for architects when seeking to communicate the design to other persons. However, the architect must pay the artist for his services which can be quite expensive. In addition, a design is often changed many times before it's approved, making the rendering or model invalid.

In recent years a new option has opened up to architects, engineers and other designers. CAD can now be used to draw a wireframe representation of the design in three dimensions on the computer. The design can then be colored and shaded right on the computer to produce a rendering.

1

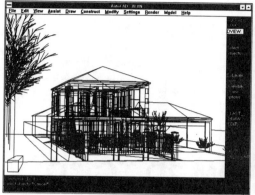 

FIGURE 1-1. A 3D drawing and rendering of a house.

With 3D CAD, a computer rendering can be produced in approximately the same time as a traditional rendering. Working in 3D also has several important advantages:

- If the architect or drafter is having difficulty visualizing some aspect of the design, a 3D drawing will make it clear.

- Technical problems which were not obvious in the 2D drawing are easier to spot in a 3D drawing.

- The architect or drafter can create the rendering in-house, provided the appropriate software is learned. This approach saves both time and money, and many computer users enjoy this artistic work.

- If the design is changed, it is much easier and cheaper to reproduce another rendering on the computer than it is to hire an artist to create another traditional rendering.

- 3D CAD can be used to create animation, where a viewer can "fly around" a building or take a tour of the interior before the design has been built.

A 3D drawing can be made in AutoCAD, while the color and animation can be added with 3D Studio. With this book you'll learn how to use these packages to make and render a 3D drawing of a design.

Although 3D drawings are useful for spotting problems and helping the designer visualize the design, its main purpose is to aid in *presentation*. In a presentation, the architect seeks to win over a client or agency, or help a client understand the design. As 3D imaging becomes more and more sophisticated, the visualizer's goal is not just to increase the client's understanding but to impress and dazzle with a visual feast.

Presentations

The purpose of a presentation is to provide all the information necessary for the client to make a decision about the design. Any method may be employed so long as it furthers the client's understanding. Presentations appear in many forms:

Simple Brochure. A simple presentation consists of 3D renderings and text assembled and printed on letter size paper. The text provides information about the design while the renderings give the reader a visual reference. The entire presentation can be assembled on an ordinary PC, printed on an office laser printer and bound with inexpensive plastic slide binding from the local stationery store. A color printer can provide color renderings, and one or more plots can be added as a technical reference. This type of presentation is inexpensive and quick to produce.

Color Brochure. Color renderings of the 3D design can be used as part of a more sophisticated presentation. Text and pictures are laid out with attention to style, and the brochure is printed by a professional printing concern. This type of presentation is more costly to produce, but when done in quantity the price per piece decreases. For this reason color brochures are most often used for mass mailing rather than individual presentations.

Onscreen Presentation. For a live presentation to a client, all drawings and renderings can be shown right on the computer screen. Text can be added to a rendering to point out areas of interest and increase clarity. A disk presentation can also be prepared so the presentation can be viewed on the client's own computer. This type of presentation is still considered rather new to architecture, and thus has a certain novelty value in itself. It has the added advantage of being producable right on a PC without any additional hardware or software.

Video. A full color animated presentation can be assembled on video to give the client a complete picture of the design. Titles and sound can be added along with your company logo. This type of presentation is very impressive but is expensive to produce in comparison other methods. The animation can be produced on your computer, but recording to video requires additional equipment (or the help of a video service) and special expertise. Still, more and more architectural offices are turning to video to win over larger clients.

A presentation may contain more than one of the elements above. A good presentation communicates the design while impressing the viewer.

Ideally you will have a firm idea of the kind of presentation you wish to use before you begin creating a 3D drawing. Since the goal of 3D work is to educate and impress the client, the form of the presentation will govern your choices in working with 3D.

Making a 3D Rendering

To make a 3D computer rendering, you must first construct the design in three dimensions in AutoCAD. Once the drawing has been made it can be rendered. In order to create a realistic rendering you will need to use a package especially for this purpose.

3D Studio is a rendering package from Autodesk, the same company that created AutoCAD. In 3D Studio you can create an entire *scene* for your drawing. For example, you can add custom decor such as wallpaper and shingles to the building and place lights anywhere you like to illuminate the design. All these elements are part of the 3D scene.

After the 3D drawing has been created in AutoCAD, it is exported to DXF format. You then load 3D Studio and import the DXF file. Lights and decor are added, and the scene is rendered from within 3D Studio.

3D CONCEPTS

Two important terms are used frequently in this book:

2D is short for *two-dimensional*. It refers to any work done with only the X and Y coordinates.
3D is short for *three-dimensional*. This term refers to drawings made with the X, Y and Z coordinates.

The Z Axis

In a 2D drawing, all entities are represented with X,Y coordinates only. With the addition of a Z coordinate a third dimension is added to the drawing.

Consider a flat object such as a sheet of paper. All points on the paper can be defined with the Cartesian axes X and Y, with X as the horizontal axis and Y as the vertical axis. In this case, the Z axis would be perpendicular to the paper, as in Figure 1-2.

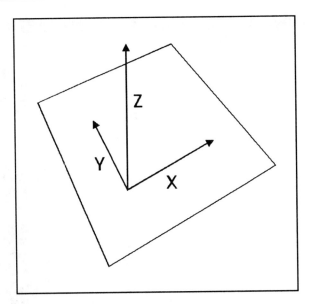

FIGURE 1-2. The Z axis.

This 3D axis performs similarly to a 2D axis. It has a point of origin (0,0,0) and Z coordinates are placed along the Z axis. In AutoCAD, if the screen holds the X,Y plane then the Z axis points into and out of the monitor. If you think of the origin as being at the lower left of your AutoCAD screen, the X-axis is toward the right, the Y-axis is toward the top, and the Z-axis is toward your eye.

In AutoCAD, if no Z coordinate is entered, the Z value is considered to be zero. However, a Z coordinate can be entered with most commands. You can see the drawing in three dimensions by changing the viewing angle of your viewport. Specific commands for working with the Z coordinate are covered in this book.

AutoCAD in 3D

A Z coordinate can be used with several AutoCAD commands to create an entity in 3D space.

For example, the LINE command can be used to create a line in 3D space.

Command: **LINE**
from point: **10, 10, 0**
to point: **50, 50, 50**
to point:

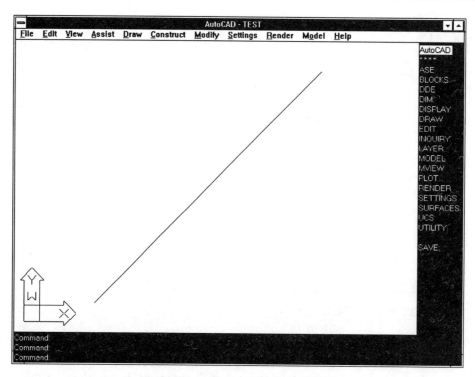

FIGURE 1-3. Line drawn in 3D space.

The 3D aspect of the line is not visible in plan view. To see the drawing's 3D dimensions, change to an angled view with the VPOINT command.

Command: **VPOINT**
Rotate/<View point> <0,0,1>:

A compass icon and an axes tripod appear. As you move your mouse, the tripod appears to spin, and a cursor moves around in the compass icon. Choose a viewpoint by manipulating whichever symbol you prefer. The compass consists of a cross-hairs and two concentric circles. The inner circle represents the "horizon line," or zero on the Z-axis. If you choose a point outside the inner circle, you will be below your object, looking up at it. If you move the cursor inside the inner circle and position it at the intersection of the cross-hairs, you will be looking straight down at your object. If the object is a building, this is known as the "plan view."

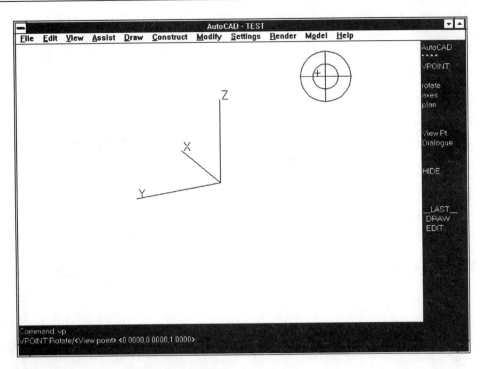

FIGURE 1-4. Compass and axes tripod.

Move the cursor to change the viewpoint. When you have a viewpoint you like, click to set the viewpoint. The screen will redraw based on your new viewpoint. With VPOINT, the target point of view is always 0,0,0.

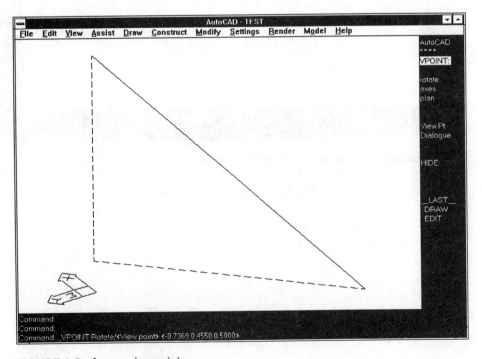

FIGURE 1-5. A new viewpoint.

Notice that the right-angle arrows symbol at the bottom left of the screen has changed appearance. This is the UCS symbol, and will be explained later.

You can also change your view angle more specifically by entering coordinates with VPOINT.

Command: **VPOINT**
Rotate/<View point> <0,0,1>: **1,1,1**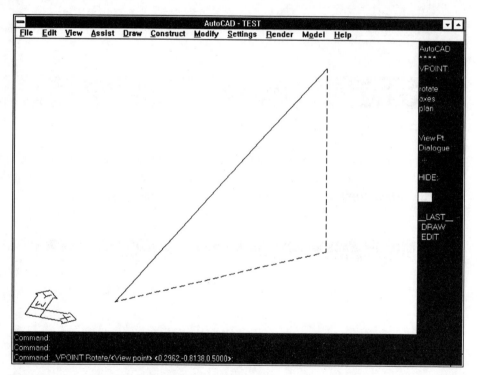

The entry 1,1,1 moves your viewing position to the angle defined by a vector going from the 1,1,1 point to the 0,0,0 point. This view causes us to look straight down our 3D line.

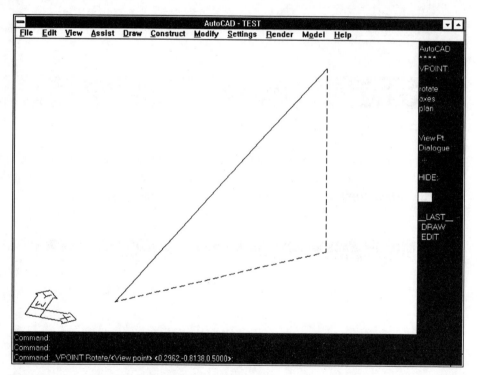

FIGURE 1-6. The view with VPOINT set to 1,1,1.

The entry 0,0,1 sets the view back to the plan view. .

Command: **VPOINT**
Rotate/<View point> <1,1,1>: **0,0,1**

Limitations

Just because a drawing is made with 3D coordinates in AutoCAD doesn't mean it can be used for rendering. A 3D drawing must be created with certain commands and procedures in order to be recognized by a rendering package.

For example, consider a cube made of simple lines (called a *wireframe*), as shown in Figure 1-7. In a rendering package this cube will not be perceived as a 3D object. A flat plane must be placed across each face of the cube in order to make it a "solid" object.

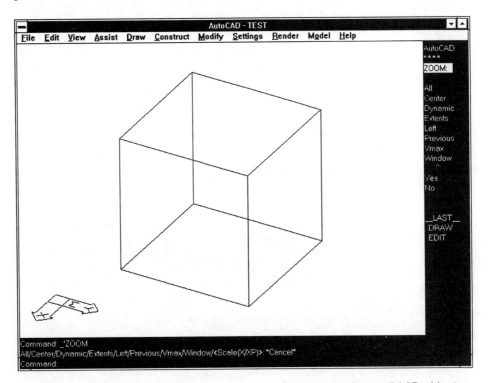

FIGURE 1-7. A series of lines make a cube, but not necessarily a solid 3D object.

The flat planes are not visible to the user but are perceived by both AutoCAD and 3D Studio. On your drawing screen, an entity created as a wireframe looks the same as one created with 3D solidity.

Whether an entity has 3D solidity depends on how it's created. Certain AutoCAD commands will create "solid" 3D entities, while others will not. In the chapters that follow you'll learn which AutoCAD commands will work for 3D.

CHAPTER

2

INTRODUCTION
TO 3D STUDIO

3D Studio is a package designed specifically for 3D visualization. A drawing in 3D Studio, called a *model*, is always three-dimensional. 3D Studio can utilize models made in AutoCAD, or you may make them from scratch in 3D Studio itself.

Once a 3D model has been created or imported to 3D Studio, the process of creating an image becomes similar to photography. Lights are placed around the model to illuminate it, and a camera is set up to create a perspective view. Different portions of the model can be colored or covered with bitmaps for the best effect.

When a scene has been set up to your satisfaction, you then tell 3D Studio to create a picture based on your settings. The process is called *rendering*. The end result of rendering is a picture of your model.

3D Studio can also be used to create an animated sequence. For example, you might want your viewers to feel they are flying around or through your model. In 3D Studio you can tell the camera to move through the model over a specified period of time, which will result in an animated sequence.

In this chapter we will discuss many aspects of 3D Studio. For reference we will also compare 3D Studio to AutoCAD. As the various parts of 3D Studio are explained, please feel free to experiment with the menu options and familiarize yourself with 3D Studio's commands.

For this chapter, load 3D Studio on your computer.

AutoCAD vs. 3D Studio

AutoCAD and 3D Studio are similar in many ways, but also have some important differences. An AutoCAD user can find 3D Studio confusing or frustrating if these differences are not fully understood.

Snap and Grid. Both AutoCAD and 3D Studio have *snap* and *grid* functions which are similar in operation. The key advantage AutoCAD has over 3D Studio is its *Object Snap* (OSNAP) mode. While drawing, you can snap directly to any point in the drawing, making drawing much easier as well as extremely accurate. 3D Studio does not have an equivalent facility.

Coordinates. In AutoCAD, any point request can be supplied with absolute, relative, cartesian or polar coordinates. While some of 3D Studio's commands will accept typed coordinates, many will not. 3D Studio is set up for a more artistic style of drawing, where object size and position are judged more by how they look than by exact coordinates. This difference can be a frustrating for an experienced AutoCAD user accustomed to typing in coordinates.

Undo. AutoCAD retains a full editing history for the current drawing session, allowing you to undo any number of steps. 3D Studio has a very limited ability to undo. A single-level undo is available in the 2D Shaper and 3D Lofter, while the 3D Editor has no undo function at all.

In its place, 3D Studio has a *hold* function which saves the current status of the 3D model in a temporary file. You can *hold* the model just before an uncertain operation, then perform a *fetch* to bring it back if necessary. When working with 3D Studio you must remember to *hold* before making a drastic change you may not want to keep. Many users find that after some experience with 3D Studio they become proficient with *hold* and *fetch* and don't miss having an undo function.

Editing. When you're editing an entity, an AutoCAD command will always ask for all the information it needs. 3D Studio assumes much of the information you're accustomed to providing with AutoCAD. For example, when rotating an entity in AutoCAD you are asked for the center of rotation and the rotation angle. In 3D Studio, the center of rotation is assumed to be the current axis which may or may not be displayed on the screen. An AutoCAD user will try to rotate an object in 3D Studio and wonder why it goes flying off the screen. As with many other differences between AutoCAD and 3D Studio, it's a matter of getting used to the way things work.

Layers and Objects. Drawings in AutoCAD are arranged by layer, while 3D Studio models are arranged by objects.

3D drawings from AutoCAD are usually imported to 3D Studio by layer. This means that a separate layer is necessary for each 3D object. For this reason, the layering system used for 2D drawing is generally not the best for a 3D drawing.

You may find it useful to create a 2D drawing in the manner to which you are accustomed, then use that 2D drawing to make a separate 3D drawing. Because the layering systems for 2D and 3D are so different, it will be difficult for you to assemble layers that are workable for both types of files.

Viewports. The 3D Studio viewport layout is more fixed than AutoCAD's. The 3D Studio default viewport layout is usually sufficient for all 3D work as the three orthogonal views define the model from every angle.

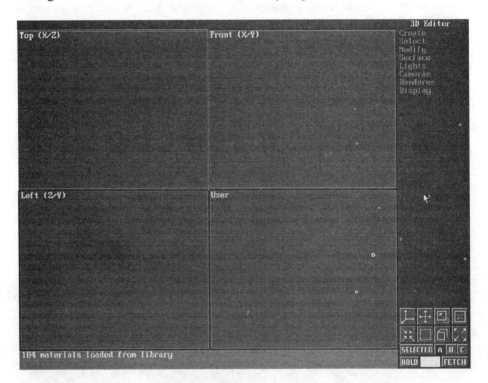

FIGURE 2-1. 3D Studio viewport layout.

Note that 3D Studio's Front viewport shows the X/Y plane. This is the equivalent of plan view in AutoCAD. The viewport labeled Top might seem more likely to show the plan view, but it shows the X/Z plane. Although 3D Studio's viewport labels might seem confusing at first, in practice most AutoCAD users find them easy to work with. Drawings brought in from AutoCAD are automatically reoriented to 3D Studio's viewports during the import process.

AutoCAD is capable of many viewport layouts, but many AutoCAD users prefer to work with one large viewport. This is practical for 2D work, but in 3D work you might find it useful to create two or more viewports on the AutoCAD screen.

Modeling

Both 3D Studio or AutoCAD can be used to make 3D models. You may wonder which program is best for modeling.

AutoCAD is designed primarily for accurate drawing. If the model must be dimensionally correct, AutoCAD should be used. All the accurate drawing tools you need will then be available and the final model will be correct. If the model has to "look" right but accurate dimensions are not important, then 3D Studio is the better choice for modeling.

Often you will find that some parts of a model are best built in AutoCAD while others should be made in 3D Studio. For example, you might make a building exterior in AutoCAD to ensure accuracy, then make the interior fixtures such as tables and lamps with 3D Studio for the most attractive presentation.

3D Studio Modules

3D Studio contains five modules. Each is used for a different part in the process of creating a 3D rendering. You can move from one module to another with the *Program* menu. To see which module you're currently in, check the upper right corner of the screen.

3D Editor. When you load 3D Studio, the 3D Editor is automatically loaded. The 3D Editor is where you will do most of your work, such as assigning materials and placing lights and cameras. You can also build objects in the 3D Editor.

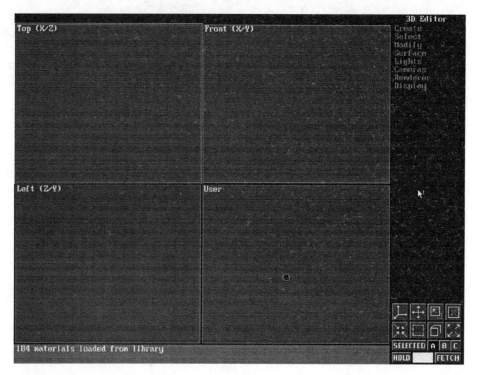

FIGURE 2-2. 3D Editor.

2D Shaper. The 2D Shaper is used to draw or import two-dimensional shapes into 3D Studio. The shapes can then be extruded in the 3D Lofter.

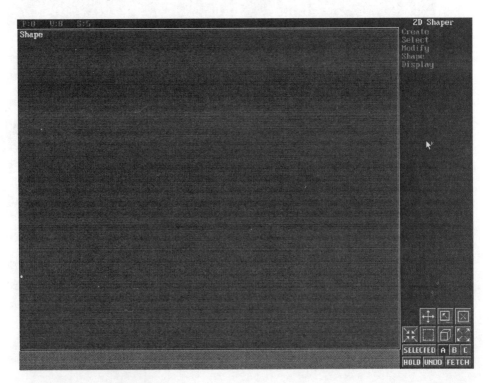

FIGURE 2-3. 2D Shaper.

The 2D Shaper contains a number of drawing tools that will be familiar to AutoCAD users. Circles, rectangles and arcs can be drawn, and in most cases coordinates can be entered directly. This module is covered in more detail in *Chapter 3*.

3D Lofter. The 3D Lofter receives polygons from the 2D Shaper, extrudes them, and sends them to the 3D Editor.

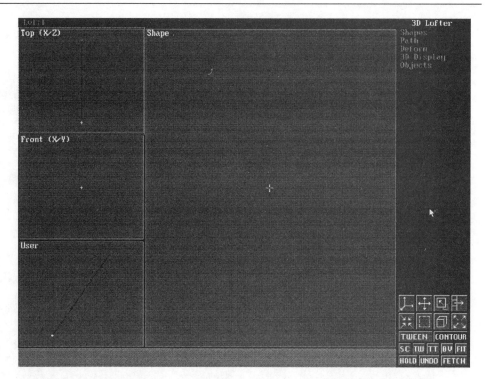

FIGURE 2-4. 3D Lofter.

Polygons are extruded along a path. The path can be straight or curved.

Materials Editor. This module is used to create and edit materials.

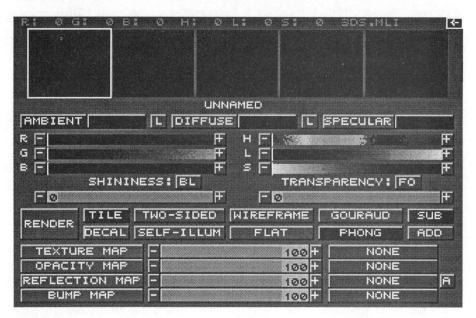

FIGURE 2-5. Materials Editor.

A material is like paint or wallpaper attached to an object. Although materials are created in the Materials Editor, they are assigned in the 3D Editor. This module is explained in more detail in *Chapters 5* and *7*.

Keyframer. The Keyframer is used to set up and render animation.

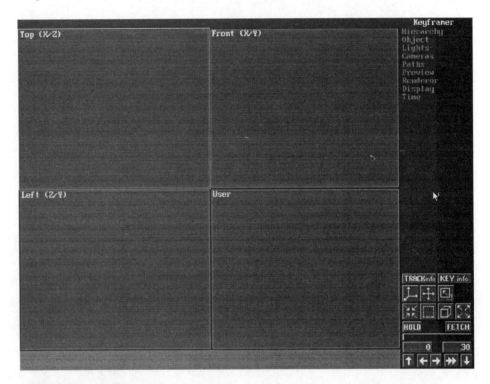

FIGURE 2-6. Keyframer.

This module is covered in more detail in *Chapter 6*.

3D STUDIO CONCEPTS

In order to use 3D Studio effectively you must understand the concepts behind it. These concepts are essential to your work in 3D Studio.

Objects

In 3D Studio, separate pieces of your model are called *objects*. An object in 3D Studio is not always the same as an entity in AutoCAD. In 3D Studio, an object is a collection of lines and points that can be picked up and moved as one solid piece. One or more AutoCAD entities become one 3D Studio object. Each object in a 3D Studio model has a unique name up to ten characters long.

As in AutoCAD, a 3D Studio object is defined as a collection of lines which designate the wireframe form of the object.

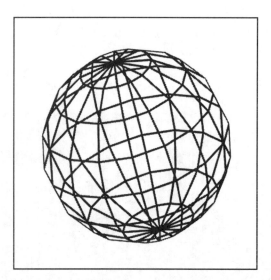

FIGURE 2-7. Wireframe representation of a sphere.

An object in 3D Studio is sometimes called a *mesh* or *mesh object*.

To create the sphere shown above, first load 3D Studio and make sure you're in the 3D Editor. To check this, look for the words **3D Editor** at the upper right corner of the screen. If you're not in the 3D Editor, press the F3 key. If this doesn't bring you to the 3D Editor, exit 3D Studio and re-enter.

Once you're in the 3D Editor, choose *Create/GSphere/Smoothed*. Click on any viewport to select it. Click near the center of the viewport to set the center of the sphere. Move the cursor to set the radius, and click to set the sphere. Enter the object name **Sphere** and click on **Create** to make the sphere.

Vertices and Faces

An object is made up of *vertices* and *faces*. Vertices is plural for *vertex*. A vertex is a point where two or more lines meet. A face is a flat plane bounded by vertices.

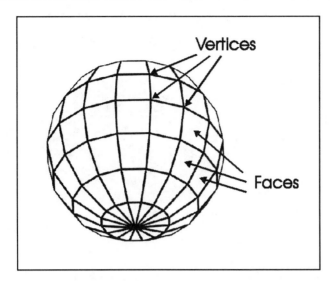

FIGURE 2-8. Vertices and faces on a sphere.

In 3D Studio, as in AutoCAD, all faces are flat. A seemingly round object such as sphere is actually made up of many flat faces. The more faces a sphere has, the more smoothly rounded it appears.

FIGURE 2-9. The top sphere has few faces, while the sphere on the bottom has many.

When you import a 3D model from AutoCAD into 3D Studio, the conversion process will automatically change your AutoCAD model to 3D Studio faces and vertices. It will also separate the drawing into objects and assign a unique name to each one.

Objects can be created in three different ways:

In AutoCAD. Objects can be made in AutoCAD and exported to DXF format. The DXF file can then be imported to 3D Studio.

In 3D Studio, in the 3D Editor. There are several object creation options under the Create menu in the 3D Editor.

In 3D Studio, from the 2D Shaper and 3D Lofter. 2D shapes (polygons) can be created in the 2D Shaper. A shape can then be extruded or revolved around an axis in the 3D Lofter, making a 3D object.

Normals

Every 3D Studio object has an "inside" and an "outside". When you create walls, for example, 3D Studio knows the walls have an inside and an outside.

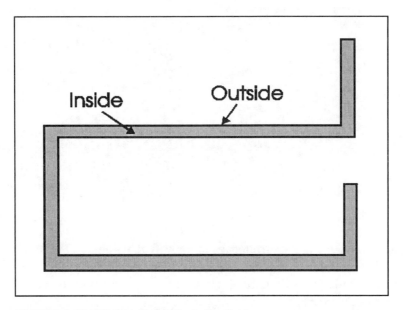

FIGURE 2-10. Walls with inside and outside.

This helps keep rendering time to a minimum, as the renderer will calculate the image based on only the "outsides" of objects. This makes sense as most of the time you won't be interested in what the insides of your objects look like. If you were to move your camera inside an object and render the view, you would see absolutely nothing. The "inside" of an object is invisible in a rendering.

3D Studio actually assigns an "inside" and "outside" to each face in the model. The "outside" is specified by an invisible arrow pointing outward and perpendicular to the face. This arrow is called a *normal*.

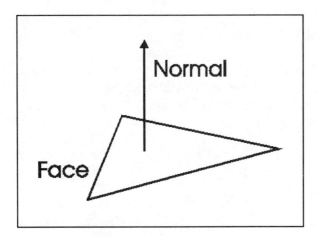

FIGURE 2-11. Normal of a face.

When you import a model from AutoCAD, 3D Studio sometimes has difficulty determining the "inside" and "outside" of objects. The result is that faces seem to be missing from the final rendering, as in the image at left in Figure 2-12.

FIGURE 2-12. 3D model with missing faces, and same model rendered with two-sided faces.

This problem is due to the differences in the way that AutoCAD and 3D Studio interpret models. Rather than trying to "flip" the normals on the offending faces, an easier solution is to tell 3D Studio to render both sides of all faces in the model. This process is explained in *Chapter 5*.

WORKING WITH COLOR

To produce a computer rendering you must apply color to a 3D drawing. Understanding how to work with color is very important when making 3D renderings.

Most of your work with color will take place in 3D Studio rather than AutoCAD. Fortunately, 3D Studio has interactive tools that make color mixing rather easy. You can change the color in a number of ways and see the color change as you work with it.

Traditional Color Wheel

Colors are treated differently by the computer and traditional media. In a traditional discipline such as paints on canvas, artists work with the primary colors red, yellow and blue. These colors can then be mixed to form orange, green and purple, as shown by the color wheel in Figure 2-13.

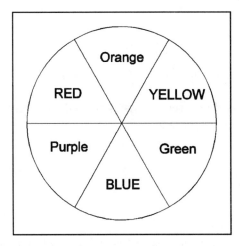

FIGURE 2-13. RYB color wheel.

The color black is produced by mixing the primary colors red, yellow and blue. Absence of any color produces white.

Computer Color Wheel

With a computer, the primary colors are red, green and blue. Secondary colors are yellow, cyan and magenta.

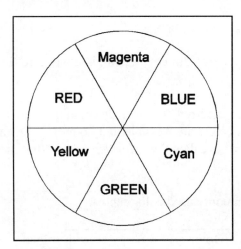

FIGURE 2-14. RGB color wheel.

With computer colors, red, greed and blue mix to form white. Black is produced with an absence of color. Note that on the computer color wheel, yellow is formed by mixing red and green. This is the color mix that is most unlike the traditional color wheel. The color cyan, a blue-green tone, is frequently seen as a computer menu color. Magenta is a reddish purple. In 3D Studio, each color is defined by its red, green and blue values. Each value can be from 0 to 255. For example, an RGB value of 255,0,0 will produce a pure red.

Color Depth

On the computer, information is stored in small areas called *bits*. Each bit can hold one of two values. These two values are commonly referred as zero and one.

The computer stores bits in groups. Each set of bits is treated as a group. A group of eight bits, for example, might look like Figure 2-15.

1	0	1	1	0	1	0	1

FIGURE 2-15. A group of eight bits.

Because bits are treated as a group, there are several possible combinations of ones and zeros.

1	0	1	1	0	1	0	1
0	1	1	0	0	0	1	0
0	1	0	1	1	1	0	1
1	0	1	0	1	0	1	1

FIGURE 2-16. Several combinations of eight bits.

In a set of eight bits, there can be 2 to the 8th power combinations. 2 to the eighth power equals 256.

The number of color bits is often referred to when discussing color. 8-bit color, for example, means that 256 different colors are possible, but no more. The amount of color possible based on the number of bits is called the *color depth*. An 8-bit image has a color depth of 256.

Refer to Table 2-17 below for commonly used color depths.

Number of bits	Calculation	Color Depth
1	2^1	2
4	2^4	16
8	2^8	256
16	2^{15}	32,768
24	2^{24}	16,777,216
32	2^{24}	16,777,216

FIGURE 2-17. Color depth table.

With 1-bit color only two colors are possible, black and white. For 16-bit color, one bit is used for other information, so the number of colors is based on the calculation 2^{15}. With 32-bit color the last eight bits are used for additional information as well, so the calculation is 2^{24}.

The number of bits is used in the computer industry to describe the capabilities of equipment. For example, a video display card might boast that it's capable of 32-bit color. A general use personal computer usually works with 8-bit color; a higher color depth is possible only with the addition of more costly equipment.

In 3D Studio, each color is defined by its RGB value. Since each of the R, G and B values can be a number from 0 to 255, there are 256 settings for each color, giving you a total of 256^3 or 16,777,216 colors. 3D Studio can also produce the extra eight bits of information used in 32-bit color, so it is capable of 32-bit color in all renderings. The number of colors you actually see on your monitor will depend on the type of display equipment you have.

Bitmaps

The term *bitmap* is used to describe an image file. This type of file consists of many dots of color (pixels) which form the picture. Each pixel is saved as a number corresponding to a specific color. When the picture is displayed on your screen, the computer decodes the numbers and displays the picture in color.

Bitmaps can be created in a number of ways. A scanned picture is saved as a bitmap on the computer. Any rendered image you create is also a bitmap.

CAD drawings are not bitmaps. A CAD drawing is saved as a collection of data on the location of points, lines and curves, not as a series of dots. To change the slope of a line in a CAD drawing, you can move the endpoint of a line and the entire line will change accordingly. With a bitmap you would have to move each pixel of the line individually.

CAD drawings are *vector* images, meaning you can change the drawing by moving endpoints. Bitmaps are *raster* images, meaning you can change the image only by changing individual pixels. A CAD drawing might be considered to be 3D if it contains 3D information, but a bitmap is always considered to be 2D as it contains only colored pixels.

Bitmaps might not seem useful to you right now, but they are vital to the more artistic aspects of 3D imaging. For example, you might want a realistic roof on your 3D building. For this purpose you can scan in a few pieces of roof tile and save the image as a bitmap file. The bitmap can then be applied to your 3D drawing for a more realistic roof. This effect would be impossible without a bitmap.

A bitmap can have any color depth from 1 to 32 bits. To change a bitmap you must use a *paint program*, a program made especially for working with bitmaps. There are many paint programs on the market today. As you venture further into 3D imaging, you may want to familiarize yourself with a paint program. This will enable you to customize your bitmaps for the best 3D renderings possible.

USING 3D STUDIO

3D Studio contains many features which may not be familiar to the AutoCAD user. Many of these items appear throughout 3D Studio and are essential to your work. As you read this section, try out the functions as described and experiment further as you like. The more comfortable you are with these functions, the better your work in 3D Studio will go.

Viewports

The 3D Editor, Keyframer and 3D Lofter all use viewports. Each viewport can be assigned a different view of your model.

In order to work in a viewport you must first make it the current viewport. This is accomplished by clicking anywhere in the viewport. The current viewport has a double line around it.

When working in 3D Editor it may sometimes seem as though a command is not working. If you are trying to work in a viewport that is not the current viewport, the first mouse click will be used to select the viewport. A second mouse click is required to activate the command.

Practice selecting viewports by clicking on each viewport. Watch for the double surrounding line that designates the current viewport.

Menus

The menu layout of the 3D Editor is very similar to that of AutoCAD. Each has a three-line command prompt area at the bottom of the screen, a set of pull-down menus across the top and commands that are accessed from a vertical menu on the right side of the screen.

The pull-down menus are active only when the cursor is moved to the top left of the screen. To see the pulldown menus, move the cursor to the top left of the screen.

FIGURE 2-18. Pull-down menus.

At all other times, a coordinate display resides in that area. AutoCAD permits custom menus to be created, but the 3D Studio menu is permanently fixed.

When you choose a menu option from the right of the screen, the command turns yellow. Further choices appear underneath the menu, indented to the right. Each submenu in 3D Studio is indented to the right of the previous menu.

Canceling Commands

A 3D Studio command remains current until you choose another command. For example, suppose you have just clicked on *Create/Box* to start making a box. The command line contains the following message:

Click to set first corner of box

The command sequence appears to have started already, but in reality the command doesn't start until you click in a viewport and start creating the box.
At this point you can simply choose another command from the menu to cancel the box creation.

When you have finished with a command, it appears to remain selected, as the first prompt for the command appears again on the command line. To "cancel" the command and start another process, simply make another choice on the menu.

If you are in the middle of an operation and wish to cancel, do a right-click with your pointing device, or choose another menu option.

Object Orientation

When you create an object with the *Create* menu, you designate the size and orientation by drawing in a viewport. For example, a cylinder is created by choosing *Create/Cylinder/Smoothed*, then clicking in any viewport. Draw a circle in the viewport. The prompt line then asks you to draw a length line.

Click in viewport to define length of cylinder:

You can specify the length of the cylinder by drawing a line in any viewport. To make a length line, click once in the viewport, then move the cursor to make a line of any length. Click to set the length of the line. You then enter a name for the cylinder object, and a cylinder is created on the screen. Figure 2-19 below illustrates this process.

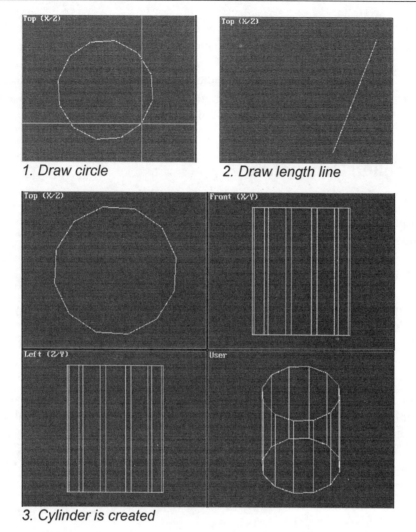

1. Draw circle   2. Draw length line

3. Cylinder is created

FIGURE 2-19. The circle and the line give 3D Studio enough information to create the cylinder.

Many objects under the *Create* menu are drawn in this way. First a 2D view of the object is drawn, then a line is drawn to represent the height of the object. The orientation of the object is set by the first drawing viewport. The Top viewport, for example, represents the X/Z plane, so an object drawn starting in the Top viewport sets the object's size and orientation along the X and Z axes.

The length line can be thought of as equivalent to *thickness* in AutoCAD, except that it's not limited to the Z axis. The length line represents the thickness along whichever axis is not represented in the drawing viewport.

For example, for an object drawn in the Top (X/Z) viewport, the length line determines the object's length along the remaining axis, Y.

To draw a length line, click in the viewport and move the cursor. A line will be drawn from the first click point. Watch the status line for the line length and move the cursor to make the line the appropriate length. Click to set the length of the line.

A length line is often confusing for AutoCAD users as it does not utilize the drawing method to which they are accustomed. If you're having trouble drawing objects, be sure to look at the command prompt at the bottom of the screen to determine the next step in the drawing process. Common mistakes are forgetting to click on the *Faceted* or *Smoothed* menu options to begin the drawing process, and accidentally canceling when it's time to draw the length line.

Construction Plane

We have already seen that the first step in drawing an object is to draw the 2D aspect of the object in one viewport. This part of the drawing process situates the object on the two axes defined by that viewport. To place the object on the third axis, 3D Studio uses something called the *construction plane*.

The construction plane can be thought of as the equivalent of the "elevation" setting in AutoCAD (do not confuse this with "Elevation View"). However, the construction plane is not limited to the Z axis. The construction plane is active on whichever axis is not represented by the drawing viewport.

For example, consider a cylinder drawn in the Top viewport. The Top viewport represents the X/Z plane. The location of the cone along the remaining axis, Y, is defined by the construction plane.

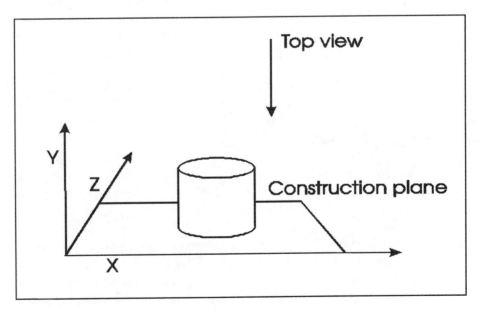

FIGURE 2-20. The construction plane for the Top viewport.

To see the construction plane, choose *Display/Const/Show*. Crosshairs will appear in each viewport. Each viewport shows the construction plane along the viewport's axes. The construction plane is defined along all three axes, but only the axis not represented by the drawing viewport is used in placing objects.

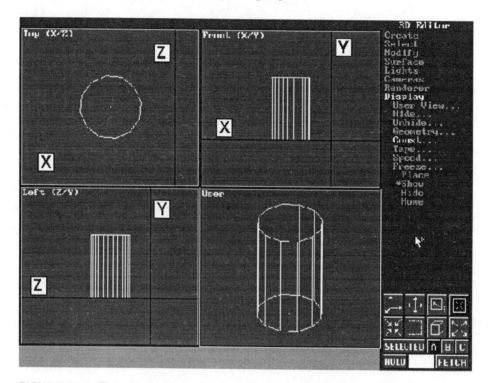

FIGURE 2-21. The construction plane is defined along all three axes.

To change the construction plane choose *Display/Const/Place* and click in any viewport to change the construction plane. Note that changing the construction plane in a viewport changes its location only along the viewport plane's axes. To change all three axes, you must change the construction plane in at least two viewports.

To hide the construction plane, choose *Display/Const/Hide*.

Object Names

When you create an object directly in 3D Studio you are prompted for an object name. The object name defaults to **Object01**, or to the name of the last object plus an incremental number. You have the option of entering a name of up to ten characters.

It is very important that you use meaningful object names in your work. An entire model composed of objects called **Object01**, **Piece02** and **Thing03** is very confusing to work with. You will find that it very hard to keep track of which object is which, and will have to constantly select and search for objects just to perform simple tasks.

When objects are created as a result of importing a DXF file, the objects are assigned names based on the AutoCAD layer names. Because we planned ahead the objects have meaningful names, making it easier to manipulate the model.

If you create any objects in 3D Studio, name them carefully so you can find them later on when you need them.

Loading and Saving Files

All file loading and saving commands can be found on the *File* menu at the top left of the screen.

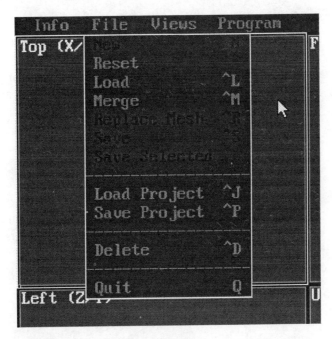

FIGURE 2-22. File menu options.

To load a mesh file, choose *Load*. A file selector appears:

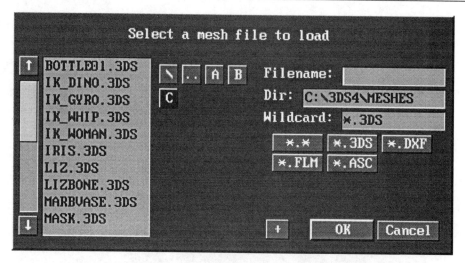

FIGURE 2-23. File selector.

The scroller on the left can be used to search through the available files. The default selection consists of files with the extension 3DS. On the right are several wildcard choices. Click on *.DXF to see the available DXF files. Click on *Cancel* to exit the dialog box without loading a file. More information on file selectors can be found in the following section.

A 3D Studio saves and loads files in the following formats:

DXF. This file format contains only 3D geometry. No lights, cameras, animation data or materials are saved. This format is useful mostly for transferring geometry from one program to another. For example, AutoCAD files are transferred to 3D Studio with the DXF format. You can also save a 3D Studio model to DXF format for transfer to another 3D program. The default subdirectory for loading and saving DXF files is the MESHES subdirectory.

3DS. This file format contains the 3D geometry, lights, camera, materials and animation data. The default subdirectory for loading and saving 3DS files is the MESHES subdirectory.

PRJ. The PRJ extension is short for *project*. A PRJ file contains 3D geometry, lights, cameras, animation data and information in the 2D Shaper, 3D Lofter and Materials Editor. The default subdirectory for loading and saving PRJ files is the PROJECTS subdirectory.

You must save to the 3DS or PRJ formats in order to keep rendering information such as lights, cameras and materials. When first starting to work with 3D Studio, use the PRJ format to make sure you keep all the necessary data. As you become more familiar with 3D Studio you'll learn whether the 3DS or PRJ format is best for your work.

To load and save 3DS files, use the *File/Load* and *File/Save* menu options. To load and save project files, use the *File/Load Project* and *File/Save Project* options.

You can also merge 3D Studio files. A merge is similar to an AutoCAD INSERT, where a model is brought in to join the current model. This option is useful for combining elements from several 3D Studio and AutoCAD models.

To merge files, choose *File/Merge*. A dialog box appears.

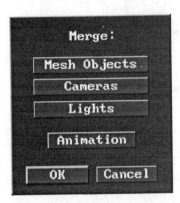

Here you can choose to bring in specific parts of a model. After you make your selections, you are prompted further for which particular objects, lights or cameras you wish to merge.

File Selectors

When working with 3D Studio you will frequently need to use file selectors similar to the ones displayed for loading and saving files. Your work with 3D Studio will go more smoothly if you learn to use the file selection buttons.

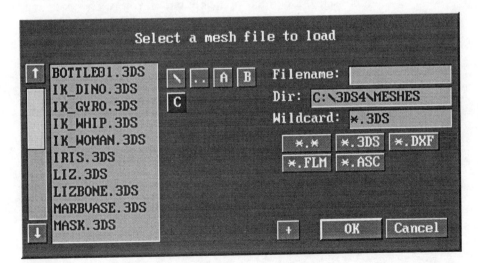

FIGURE 2-24. File selector.

Each file selector contains a similar set of buttons.

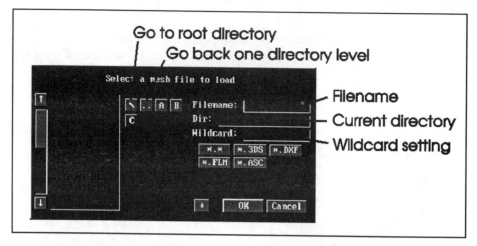

FIGURE 2-25. File selector buttons.

The filename, current directory and wildcard selection are at the right. Use the buttons at the center to choose the appropriate directory, or type it in. Use the wildcard selection buttons to choose the wildcard, or type it in.

On the left is the list of files designated by the wildcard which reside in the current directory. If more than ten files are selected, use the scroll bar at the left to look through the list of files. To select a file you can click on the file name and click on OK, or double-click on the file name.

If you're having trouble finding a file, check the following:

- The appropriate subdirectory is selected.
- The appropriate wildcard is selected.
- You have chosen the correct menu option. If you're trying to load a PRJ file, for example, and you choose *File/Load* instead of *File/Project*, the file selector will display 3DS files rather than PRJ files.

You can practice using file selectors by choosing *File/Load* or *File/Load Project*.

Zooming

Like AutoCAD, 3D Studio has commands for zooming in and out of a drawing. The zoom buttons are located at the bottom right of the screen.

Button	Name	AutoCAD Equivalent
	Zoom Extents	Zoom E, then Zoom 0.8X
	Zoom In	Zoom 2X
	Zoom Out	Zoom 0.5X
	Pan	Pan
	Zoom Window	Zoom W

FIGURE 2-26. Zoom buttons.

If you click on a zoom icon, the zoom affects only the current viewport. If you right-click on a zoom icon, the zoom affects all viewports.

To try out the zoom commands, load a 3D Studio file. From the *File* menu, choose *Load*. Locate the file CAFETABL.3DS and choose it from the file selector. Practice using the zoom commands until you're comfortable with them. Leave the file CAFETABL.3DS on the screen so you can use it to practice other commands.

Lights

In order to render a model, lights must be placed in the scene. 3D Studio has two types of lights, *omni* and *spotlight*. Omni lights shine in all directions while spotlights shine in one direction only. Shadows can be cast by spotlights only. A third type of lighting, *ambient* light, covers the entire scene uniformly.

A light in a 3D Studio scene is represented by a yellow icon. The light icons do not appear in a rendering.

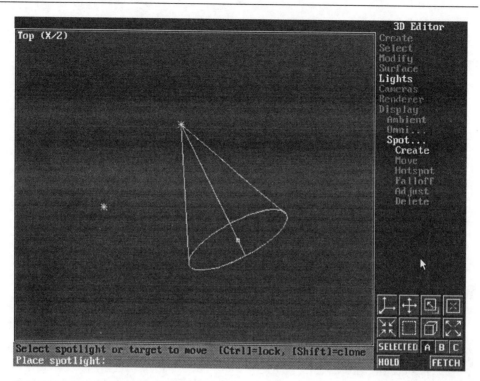

FIGURE 2-27. Omni and spotlight icons.

Lights can be placed in any position in 3D space and can have various intensities and colors. When the scene is rendered, 3D Studio calculates what the objects in the scene will look like based on the light settings. Bright lights can be used to create highlights and focus the viewer's attention on a particular portions of the model. Dimmer lights are used to fill in dark areas of the scene without distracting from the focus of the scene.

Lights are created and changed with the commands under the *Lights* menu option in the 3D Editor or Keyframer.

Cameras

In 3D Studio a *camera* is used to set up a perspective view of a model. A camera in 3D Studio works similarly to a camera in real life. It can be placed anywhere in a scene and can have any one of a variety of lens lengths.

After placing a camera in a scene you can change one of the viewports to show the camera view. When you loaded the file CAFETABL.3DS, the lower right viewport changed to the camera view.

The camera is represented as a blue icon with a direction vector. To see all current cameras, click on the *Cameras* menu option.

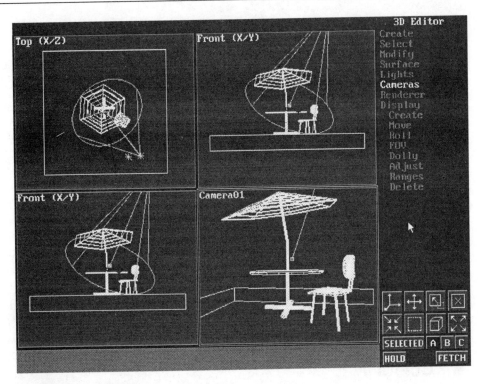

FIGURE 2-28. Camera icon.

Cameras are created and manipulated with the commands under the *Cameras* menu option in the 3D Editor and Keyframer.

TAB Key

When performing operations such as moving and scaling objects, you can set a directional arrow to restrict the operation. For example, while moving an object you can restrict the motion to the horizontal direction only.

When you choose a moving or scaling operation, an omnidirectional arrow appears in the current viewport. You can press the **TAB** key to toggle through the three directional arrows.

To try the omnidirectional arrows, go to the 3D Editor. Choose *Modify/Object/Move* and click on any viewport to make it the current viewport. While the cursor is in the current viewport, the omnidirectional arrow appears on the screen. Press the **TAB** key to toggle between the choices. When you click on an object, the movement will be limited to the direction of the arrow.

Local Axis

In the 3D Editor, rotation of an object takes place around an axis. In AutoCAD a rotation axis is set during the command sequence, but in the 3D Editor this axis must be set before using the *Rotate* command.

When you first load 3D Studio, the axis is set to the origin point. You can set the axis to a new point with the commands under *Modify/Axis*. You can also temporarily set the axis to the center of the object by turning on the **Local Axis** button.

This button appears at the lower right of the 3D Editor screen. When turned on, all rotation takes place around the center of the object.

In the Keyframer, an object's rotation axis is called its *pivot point*. The pivot point defaults to the center of the object. To change the pivot point, choose *Hierarchy/Place Pivot*, click on the object and click in one or more viewports to set the new pivot point.

Colors

There are many commands in 3D Studio that use colors. A few of the places you will encounter colors are:

Materials. The color of the material is specified in the Materials Editor.
Lights. Lights can be any color.
Background. Colors are specified for a plain color or gradient background.

In 3D Studio, colors are set up with sliders.

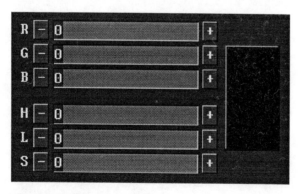

FIGURE 2-29. Color slider.

The R, G and B sliders refer to the red, green and blue values of the color. Each slider can have a value from 0 to 255. You can change the color by moving one or more sliders. The color change appears immediately in the box at the right as you change the sliders.

Below the R, G and B sliders there are three more sliders, H, L and S. When you move the R, G or B sliders, the H, L and S sliders change as well. These three sliders provide an alternate method of changing a color.

H refers to *hue*. Hue refers to the color in general, such as red, orange, yellow, green, cyan, blue or purple. As you move the slider it passes through each color in the rainbow.

Luminance is the lightness or darkness of the color. A high luminance means the color approaches white. For example, a red hue with a high luminance produces pink. A lower luminance creates a deep red. To make a light gray, increase the luminance and leave all the other sliders as they are.

Saturation refers to the brightness of the color. By brightness we mean how "hot" the color is. For example, pink with a high saturation becomes hot pink, while a low saturation produces a pastel pink.

You only need one set of sliders to define a color. For example, the RGB combination 208, 128, 12 will always produce the same HLS combination 25, 110, 227. For simplicity, when a color is specified in this book you will see only the RGB combination.

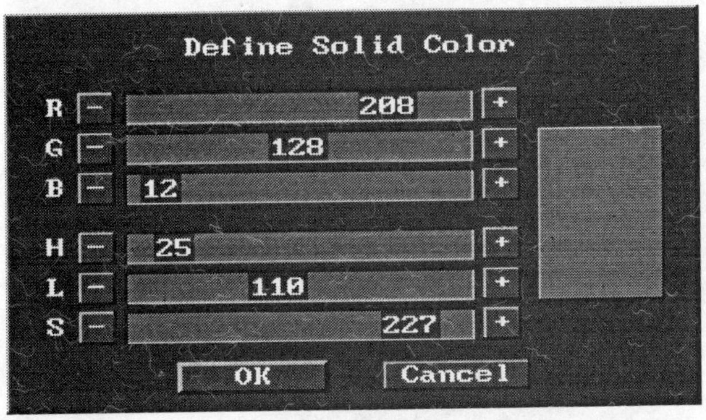

FIGURE 2-30. RGB color combination 208, 128, 12.

A few common hue combinations are as follows.

	R	G	B
Red	255	0	0
Green	0	255	0
Blue	0	0	255
Yellow	255	255	0
Orange	255	130	0
Purple	130	0	255
Black	0	0	0
White	255	255	255

FIGURE 2-31. RGB color combinations.

Because color sliders are used so often in 3D Studio, it's a good idea to become proficient at setting colors. Practice with colors by changing the background color. Choose *Renderer/Setup/Background*. A dialog box appears.

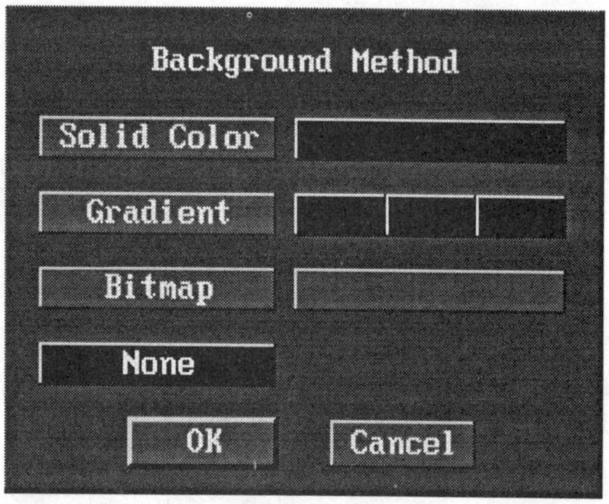

FIGURE 2-32. Background dialog box.

Click on the blank space next to **Solid Color**. A color slider appears.

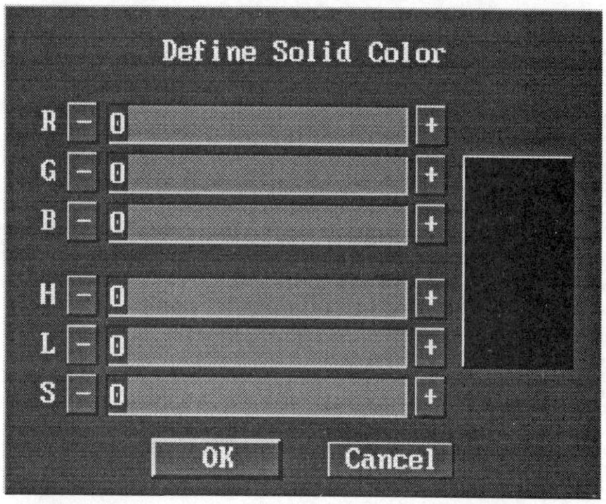

FIGURE 2-33. Color slider for solid background color.

Practice using these sliders to get a feel for how they work. When setting up colors, you may find this sequence useful:

- Use the **R, G** and **B** sliders to get the general hue. Use the RGB color wheel (Figure 2-14) and the table above to approximate the hue.
- Use the **L** slider to make the color lighter or darker as desired.
- Use the **S** slider to make the color more or less "hot".

In working with computer renderings, it's best to use colors with a saturation of less than 255. A common beginner's mistake is to make all colors extremely bright because you want the rendering to "stand out". A rendering containing highly saturated colors ends up looking like a cartoon. If you want to get your rendering noticed, go for a greater degree of realism. In life, very few colors are highly saturated.

How a color appears in your final rendering depends a great deal on your lighting setup, your video display and several other factors. For this reason, two persons using the same color values on two different computers can end up with different results. A client may try to give you specific color values to use in a rendering, but in the end you must judge and adjust the colors yourself.

Materials

Materials in 3D Studio are like a veneer covering each object. A material can be a plain color, such as red paint or blue plastic. A material can also use one or more bitmaps to make a textured pattern such as wallpaper, shingles or wood.

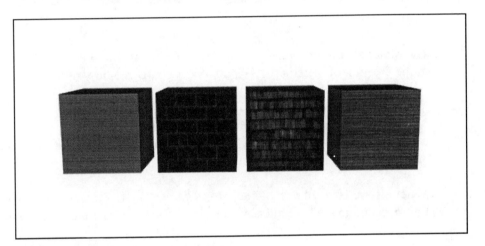

FIGURE 2-34. Paint, wallpaper, shingles and wood.

Materials are created and edited in the Materials Editor module of 3D Studio. To access the Materials Editor, choose *Materials* from the *Program* menu in any module.

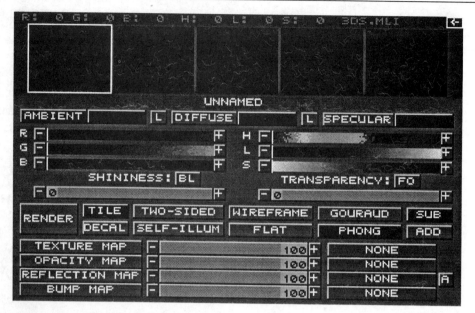

FIGURE 2-35. Materials Editor.

The Materials Editor screen may seem confusing at first. Each part plays a specific role in the creation of materials. As you work with 3D Studio you'll find that you use some settings more than others.

3D Studio comes with a set of premade materials. In many cases a premade material will work for some part of your model. These materials also provide an excellent base for more intricate materials you create yourself.

Materials are covered in more detail in *Chapter 5*. If you are currently in the Materials Editor, return to the 3D Editor by choosing *3D Editor* from the *Program* menu.

Rendering

In 3D Studio you must choose the viewport to render. Most often this will be the camera viewport, but there may be occasions where you want to render a different viewport.

During the rendering procedure, 3D Studio calculates how the model will look based on the lighting and other factors. The amount of time this takes depends on the complexity of your model and the speed of your computer. An average rendering time is 5 to 20 minutes, although rendering times of two hours are not uncommon for very complex models.

Rendering is accomplished with the commands under the *Renderer* menu option.

AUTOCAD TO 3D STUDIO

An AutoCAD drawing can be brought into 3D Studio in one of two ways.

● 2D drawings representing the plan and elevations can be brought into the 2D Shaper and lofted with the 3D Lofter to make 3D objects. This procedure is described in detail in *Chapter 3*.

● The model can be built completely in 3D in AutoCAD and brought into the 3D Editor as a complete 3D model. This process is covered in *Chapter 4*.

Both of these methods are valid. The method you choose will depend on the model and the type of objects involved. Sometimes both techniques are used on one drawing. Both methods are explored in detail in the following chapters.

To bring an AutoCAD drawing into 3D Studio, you must first export the drawing to DXF format. The DXF file can then be loaded into 3D Studio.

EXERCISES

Exercise 1

Load the 3D Studio file CAFETABL.3DS. Move the lights with the *Lights/Omni/Move* command. Move the camera with the *Cameras/Move* command and observe the result in the camera viewport.

Exercise 2

Render the camera view of CAFETABLE.3DS. To do this, choose *Renderer/Render* and click twice on the camera viewport. When the **Render Still Image** dialog box appears, click on **Render**. The image will take a few minutes to render, then will appear on the screen. Press **ESC** to return to the 3D Editor.

• • • • • • • • • • • • • • • •

CHAPTER

3

AUTOCAD PLANS
FOR 3D STUDIO

• • • • • • • • • • • • • • •

There are two ways to work with an AutoCAD drawing in 3D Studio. You can bring an AutoCAD plan into the 2D Shaper and loft it, or bring the completed 3D model into 3D Studio. In this chapter we'll look at how to make and export an AutoCAD plan to the 2D Shaper for lofting.

AUTOCAD DRAWINGS

In order to use 3D Studio to loft a plan made in AutoCAD, certain rules must be observed. In this chapter we'll look at the right way to create a plan for export, and cover a few of the wrong ways for you to avoid in your drawings.

Loftable Plan

When 3D Studio lofts a plan, it extrudes it upward to form solid walls. In order to loft successfully, the plan must be represented with closed lines. These lines must outline the "silhouette" of the plan as in Figure 3-1.

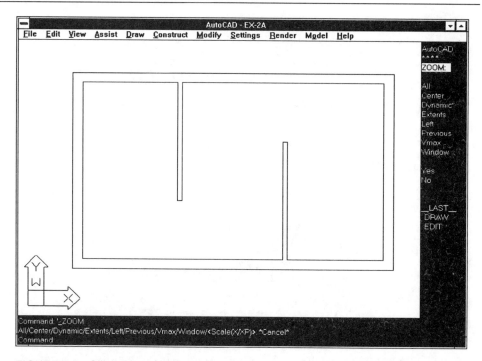

FIGURE 3-1. Silhouette of walls in plan view.

3D Studio has drawing functions to draw such a plan, but you will probably find it more practical to draw the plan in AutoCAD. If you assemble all the relevant plan drawings in AutoCAD, you'll find it easier to maintain the correct measurements along with high accuracy.

In order to be lofted in 3D Studio, an AutoCAD plan must define the solidity of the walls visually. All that is needed is one line for the outer wall and one or more lines for the inner walls.

The only lines allowed in a loftable plan are lines to define the silhouette of the plan or wall. Any other type of plan will not work. For example, the drawings in Figure 3-2 are not loftable in 3D Studio.

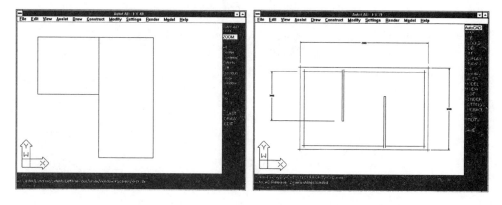

FIGURE 3-2. Non-loftable plans.

In the drawing at left, the wall outlines do not define the walls but define the entire room as a solid block. In the drawing at the right, the wall lines overlap, giving no clear indication of the exact wall outlines. In addition, measurement lines have been left in the drawing. A loftable plan must outline the walls without overlapping or extraneous lines.

To visualize a loftable plan, imagine that you have built a small clay model of your building. If you remove the roof and floor, you are left with just the walls. If you place the model on a piece of paper and trace both the outer and inner outline, the resulting drawing would be loftable in 3D Studio.

Loftable Elevation

You can also use 3D Studio to loft a wall from an elevation view. The outline of the walls can be drawn in AutoCAD, complete with holes for the windows and doors. The AutoCAD drawing can then be brought into 3D Studio for extrusion into a wall with a thickness. This is the easiest way to create a wall with holes for windows and doors.

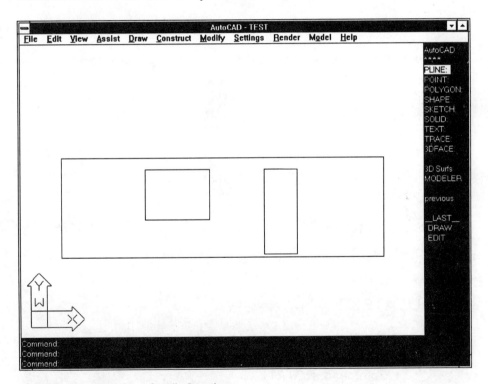

FIGURE 3-3. Drawing of wall elevation.

Like the plan, the wall outline must be made up of closed polygons. In this case two rectangular polygons are embedded inside the outline to designate window holes.

Drawing a Loftable Plan or Elevation

For best results, all lines should be drawn with PLINEs. Each line can be drawn on a separate layer, but this is not necessary.

Each polygon must be closed. Polygons may be embedded inside other polygons, but may not overlap.

In general, an architectural plan drawn for informational purposes must be changed in order to be loftable. Overlapping lines, text and unnecessary entities should be removed. The outline of the floor or wall, plus any lines to define cutouts, are all that you need.

For a loftable elevation, it makes sense to draw the elevated view in the appropriate location and orientation in 3D space. Usually the elevation belongs on the X/Z or Y/Z plane. This presents a problem, however, when the plan is exported to a DXF file and imported to 3D Studio. When a plan is imported for lofting, 3D Studio interprets the X/Y plane only.

For this reason, an elevation must be rotated into the X/Y plane after being drawn.

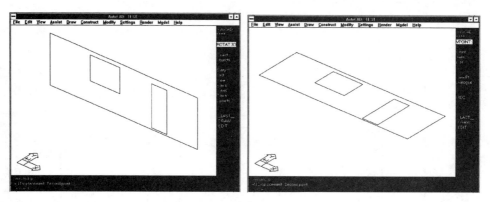

FIGURE 3-4. Wall elevation rotated into X/Y plane.

ROTATE3D

The ROTATE3D command can be used to rotate the elevation into the X/Y plane.

```
Command: ROTATE3D
Initializing...
Select objects: (Pick objects)
Select objects: ⏎
Axis by Entity/Last/View/Xaxis/Yaxis/Zaxis/<2points>: X
Point on X axis <0,0,0>: (Pick a point)
<Rotation angle>/Reference: 90
```

As with all AutoCAD commands, the entities to be rotated are selected first. Then the axis about which the entities will be rotated is entered, and a point is picked on the axis. The UCS icon is helpful in determining the appropriate axis.

Next the degrees of rotation are specified. In the case of an elevation, 90 degrees is appropriate.

Sometimes it's hard to tell whether the object should be rotated by 90 or -90 degrees. If you pick the wrong direction, the entities will rotate "down" and not "up". In this case you can either rotate the entities again by 180 degrees, or UNDO and reuse the ROTATE3D command with the appropriate degrees entry.

DXF EXPORT

Once a plan has been drawn, it must be exported to DXF format, then imported to 3D Studio. The DXFOUT command is used to export AutoCAD drawings.

Command: **DXFOUT**

You can also choose *File / Import/Export / DXFOUT* from the menu.

A dialog box appears where you can choose a subdirectory to save the DXF file.

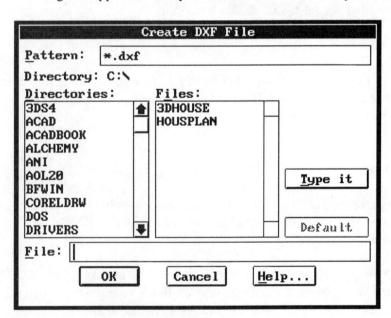

FIGURE 3-5. DXF output dialog box.

For plans to be lofted in 3D Studio, choose your 3D Studio SHAPES directory. You can also enter an output filename on this dialog box. When you exit this dialog box, the command line takes over again.

Enter decimal places of accuracy (0 to 16)/Entities/Binary <6>: **B** ⟵

DXF files may be output as ASCII or binary files. Binary files are smaller in size and load more quickly into 3D Studio, so binary format is recommended. Entering a B at the last command prompt will output the DXF file in binary format.

You also have the option of entering a number of decimal places for ASCII format. An ASCII file can be edited directly if you later find errors in the drawing. However, this is usually not necessary.

3D STUDIO LOFTING

Once the plan or drawing has been made in AutoCAD and exported to DXF format, it can be imported to 3D Studio and lofted into a 3D object.

Import to 3D Studio

To import the drawing to 3D Studio:

- Load 3D Studio.
- Go to the 2D Shaper. Choose the *Program* menu and select *2D Shaper*.
- Choose the *File* menu and select *Load*. A file selector appears.
- Click on the *.DXF wildcard selector.
- Locate the subdirectory in which the DXF file was saved.
- Choose the file.

Messages will appear at the top of screen giving the status of the import process. After a few moments, the drawing will appear on the screen. The image on the screen represents the X/Y plane of the AutoCAD drawing.

2D Shapes

A polygon in the 2D Shaper is called a *shape*. Any polygon in the 2D Shaper is treated as a shape regardless of whether it was drawn in the 2D Shaper or imported from AutoCAD.

The 2D Shaper can hold a number of shapes. Mostly likely your 2D Shaper drawing contains a set of shapes for one plan or wall. But if your drawing contains more than one set of lofting shapes, you will have to designate which shapes to use when lofting.

A set of lofting shapes is grouped with the *Shape/Assign* command. This option allows you to select only specific shapes for lofting.

For example, suppose you have imported a DXF file with two wall drawings.

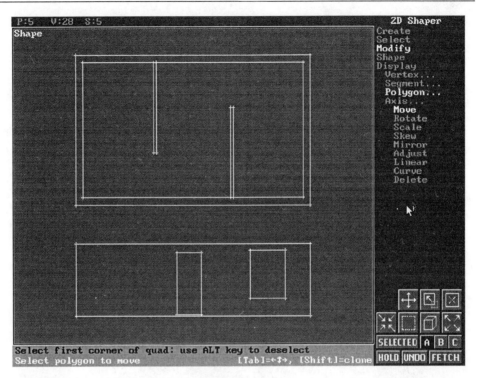

FIGURE 3-6. Two wall shapes in the 2D Shaper.

You'll want to work with one set of wall shapes at a time. In this case you'd choose *Shape/Assign* and click on the two polygons on the left. This operation tells 3D Studio that these two shapes are the ones you want to work with currently. When shapes are assigned, they turn yellow in the 2D Shaper.

If you want to use all the shapes in the 2D Shaper, it is not necessary to assign shapes.

Lofting

Lofting is accomplished by bringing a drawing (shape) from the 2D Shaper into the 3D Lofter module and extruding it along a path.

To begin the lofting process, go to the 3D Lofter by choosing *Program/3D Lofter*. To bring in the shape, choose *Shapes/Get/Shaper*. This choice brings the assigned shapes from the 2D Shaper to the 3D Lofter. If no shapes have been assigned in the 2D Shaper, all shapes in the 2D Shaper will be imported.

The shapes appear in the Shape viewport. In the Top viewport you will see a path. This is the default path for extrusion of the shapes.

The path has a unit length which determines the thickness of the extruded shape. To set the path to the desired extrusion thickness, choose *Path/Move Vertex*. Click on the Top viewport to make it the current viewport. Press the **TAB** key to change to up-down arrows. Click on the uppermost vertex on the path and move it up or down. Watch the status line at the top of the screen to see the path length change. Click to set the new path length.

The default unit of measure is the decimal inch. You will usually want to work in a unit common to your profession. Units are configured by choosing the V*iews* menu from the top of the screen, and choosing *Unit Setup*. The menu in Figure 3-7 appears. Select a format, unit value, and denominator. For example: selecting architectural, 1 unit = 1 in., denominator 4, sets the units to feet and inches, with the smallest dimension shown being 1/4 inch.

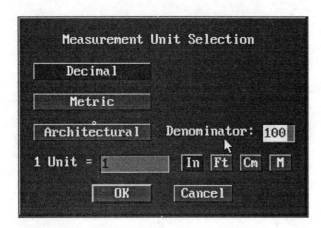

FIGURE 3-7. Unit setup.

When changing the path length you may find it difficult to accurately get the correct length. Remember that in 3D Studio a high degree of accuracy is generally not necessary. If a wall or floor is slightly thicker or thinner than specified, it will not be noticeable in the final rendering. When setting the path length go for the most accurate number possible and don't worry about the discrepancy.

When the path has been set to the appropriate length, loft the object by choosing *Object/Make*. The following dialog box appears:

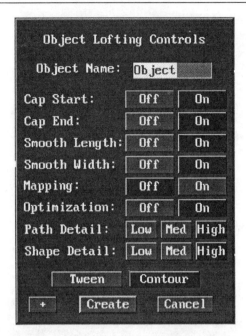

FIGURE 3-8. Dialog box for lofting shapes.

This dialog box has many options. In most cases the default settings will work fine.

Enter an object name and click on **Create** to create the object. The object will not appear in the 3D Lofter; it is created in the 3D Editor. Choose *Program/3D Editor* to move to the 3D Editor and see the object.

Rotate to Position

Once a plan has been lofted in 3D Studio it will be lying on the X/Y plane in 3D Studio (see Figure 3-10). Recall that the X/Y plane in 3D Studio is the Front view, not the Top view. This means the lofted plan will appear to be lying on its side in the 3D Editor. Note that this happens only with 2D plans, not with 3D entities imported from AutoCAD. You will have to rotate the drawing in 3D Studio to give it the proper orientation.

In 3D Studio, all rotation takes place around a preset rotation axis. You can set the axis manually by placing it in the scene, or can use 3D Studio commands to snap the axis to the center or corner of any object.

To snap the axis to center or corner, use the *Modify/Axis/Align/Object* command. Click on an object, and a dialog box appears.

FIGURE 3-9. Dialog box for aligning axis.

You can snap the rotation axis to any corner of the object, or to the center of any of the sides of the object. When preparing to rotate an object, work out where the rotation axis should be placed, and use the appropriate setting.

After the axis has been placed, it appears on the screen as a small X.

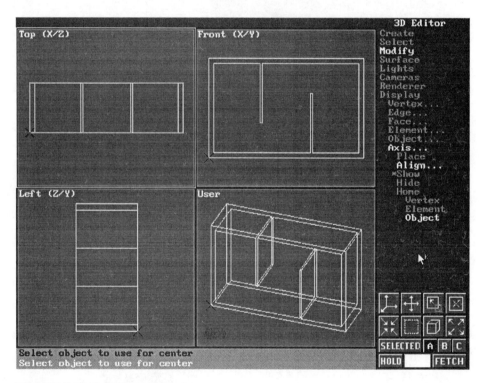

FIGURE 3-10. Axis on screen

Note that when you click on an object in a particular viewport to set the axis, it is set only along the axes represented by that viewport. For example, if you click on the object in the Top (X/Z) viewport, the rotation axis is set only for the X and Z directions.

To set the rotation point on all three axes, you must set it in at least two viewports. To do this, simply set the rotation axis twice in succession, each time in different viewports.

You can also control the rotation axis with the Local Axis button. This button appears at the lower right corner of the 3D Editor. When turned on, all rotation on an object takes place around the center of the object. When the button is turned off, rotation takes place around the rotation axis defined earlier.

Summary

One way to make a 3D model of a building in 3D Studio is to make a 2D plan or elevation drawing in AutoCAD and import it to 3D Studio for extrusion. In 3D Studio, extrusion is called lofting.

This procedure follows this sequence:

- Draw a 2D plan or elevation in AutoCAD with PLINEs.
- Export the drawing to DXF format with the DXFOUT command.
- In 3D Studio, go to the 2D Shaper. Load the DXF file with the *File/Load* command. The drawing has now become a set of 3D Studio shapes.
- Assign shapes if necessary.
- Go to the 3D Lofter. Bring in the shapes with the *Shapes/Get/Shaper* option. Adjust the path length to the extrusion thickness.
- Loft the shapes into a 3D object with the *Object/Make* command.
- Go to the 3D Editor to see the object.

TUTORIALS

These tutorials illustrate how to make a plan or wall elevation in AutoCAD for use in 3D Studio.

Tutorial 1

In this tutorial, you'll draw the floor plan below using PLINEs.

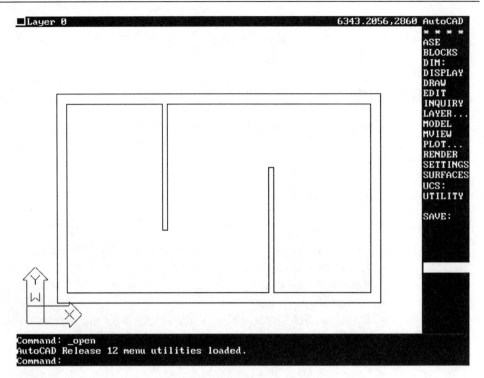

FIGURE 3-11. Plan outline.

Use the commands described below. When you've finished the drawing, you'll export it to a DXF file, import it to 3D Studio, and loft the walls.

1. Layer

First, create a layer for the walls.

> Command: **LAYER**
> ?/Make/Set/New/ON/OFF/Color/Ltype/Freeze/Thaw/LOck/Unlock: **M**
> New current layer <0>: **WALLS**
> ?/Make/Set/New/ON/OFF/Color/Ltype/Freeze/Thaw/LOck/Unlock: **C**
> Color: **RED**
> Layer name(s) for color 1 (red) <WALLS>: **WALLS**
> ?/Make/Set/New/ON/OFF/Color/Ltype/Freeze/Thaw/LOck/Unlock:

2. Outer Wall

Next you'll create the outer wall shown below.

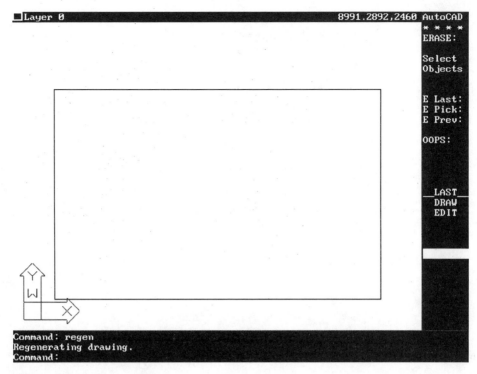

FIGURE 3-12. Outer wall.

> Command: **PLINE**
> From point: **0,0**
> Current line-width is **0.00**
> Arc/Close/Halfwidth/Length/Undo/Width/<Endpoint of line>: **@8000<0**
> Arc/Close/Halfwidth/Length/Undo/Width/<Endpoint of line>: **@5000<90**
> Arc/Close/Halfwidth/Length/Undo/Width/<Endpoint of line>: **@8000<180**
> Arc/Close/Halfwidth/Length/Undo/Width/<Endpoint of line>: **C**

The outer wall has been drawn. Zoom out to get a look at the drawing.

> Command: **ZOOM**
> All/Center/Dynamic/Extents/Left/Previous/Vmax/Window/<Scale(X/XP)>:
>   **E**
> Regenerating drawing.

> Command: **ZOOM**
> All/Center/Dynamic/Extents/Left/Previous/Vmax/Window/<Scale(X/XP)>:
>   **0.9X**

3. Inner Wall

Now you'll create the inner wall.

> Command: **PLINE**
> From point: **250,250**

Current line-width is 0.00
Arc/Close/Halfwidth/Length/Undo/Width/<Endpoint of line>: **@5000<0**
Arc/Close/Halfwidth/Length/Undo/Width/<Endpoint of line>: **@3000<90**
Arc/Close/Halfwidth/Length/Undo/Width/<Endpoint of line>: **@110<0**
Arc/Close/Halfwidth/Length/Undo/Width/<Endpoint of line>: **@3000<270**
Arc/Close/Halfwidth/Length/Undo/Width/<Endpoint of line>: **@2390<0**
Arc/Close/Halfwidth/Length/Undo/Width/<Endpoint of line>: **@4500<90**
Arc/Close/Halfwidth/Length/Undo/Width/<Endpoint of line>: **@5000<180**
Arc/Close/Halfwidth/Length/Undo/Width/<Endpoint of line>: **@3000<270**
Arc/Close/Halfwidth/Length/Undo/Width/<Endpoint of line>: **@110<180**
Arc/Close/Halfwidth/Length/Undo/Width/<Endpoint of line>: **@3000<90**
Arc/Close/Halfwidth/Length/Undo/Width/<Endpoint of line>: **@2390<180**
Arc/Close/Halfwidth/Length/Undo/Width/<Endpoint of line>: **C**

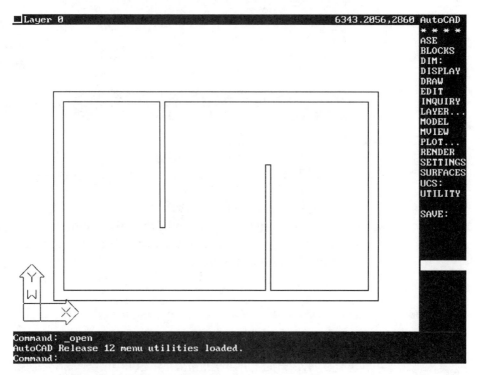

FIGURE 3-13. Complete plan drawing.

4. Save the Drawing

It's a good idea to save the drawing before exporting to a DXF file.

Command: **SAVE**
Save current changes as: **HOUSPLAN**
Current drawing name set to HOUSPLAN

5. Export to DXF File

The plan can now be output to a DXF file.

Command: **DXFOUT**
(Choose the 3D Studio SHAPES directory. Enter the name **HOUSPLAN**.)
Enter decimal places of accuracy (0 to 16)/Entities/Binary <6>: **B**

6. Import to 3D Studio

In 3D Studio, go to the 2D Shaper module. To do this, choose the *Program* pulldown menu and choose *2D Shaper*.

Load the DXF file into the 2D Shaper. To do this, choose the *File* pulldown menu and choose *Load*. Click on the *.DXF wildcard field.

Locate the subdirectory where HOUSPLAN.DXF is located. Choose HOUSPLAN.DXF.

The plan you drew in steps 3 and 4 appears on the screen.

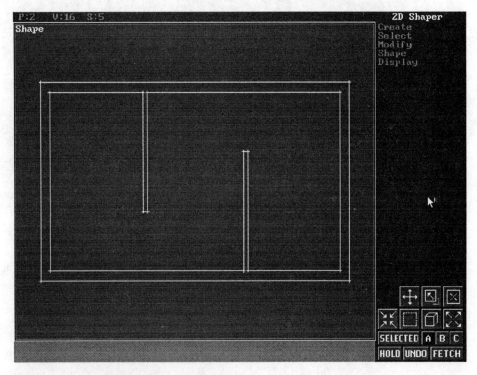

FIGURE 3-14. Plan drawing in 2D Shaper.

7. Import Shapes to 3D Lofter

Go to the 3D Lofter by choosing *Program/3D Lofter*. Choose *Shape/Get/Shaper*. The following message appears:

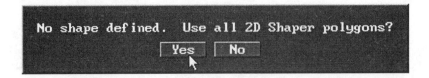

Click on **Yes**. The drawing appears in all four viewports.

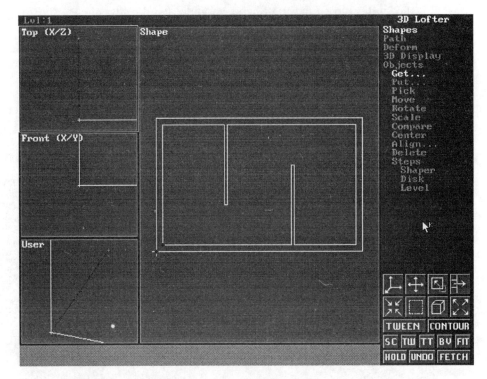

FIGURE 3-15. Plan in 3D Lofter.

Right-click on **Zoom Extents**. The path length determines how high the walls will be lofted. In the Top viewport you can see that the path length will not be long enough. For this reason you must make a new path.

Set a snap spacing to help draw the correct length line for the new path. From the pull-down menus, choose Views, then Drawing Aids. In the Drawing Aids dialogue box, enter a value of **100** in the X, Y, and Z fields under Snap Spacing. Choose **OK**.

Next, press the S key. A yellow letter **S** will appear in the upper right corner of the screen, indicating that snap is now in effect. Snap can be toggled on and off in the various modules by pressing the **S** key.

8. Draw Path

Go back to the 2D Shaper. Use *Create/Line* to draw a line 2500 units long. Watch the top of the screen to see the length of the line.

Choose *Shapes/Assign/None* to unassign all shapes, then choose *Shapes/Assign* and click on the line you just drew.

Go to the 3D Lofter. Choose *Path/Get/Shaper*. A message appears:

Click on **OK**. The line you drew will be brought in as the new path.

9. Loft Walls

Choose *Object/Make*. The following dialog box appears.

```
           Object Lofting Controls

       Object Name:  Object

  Cap Start:            Off       On
  Cap End:             Off       On
  Smooth Length:       Off·      On
  Smooth Width:        Off       On
  Mapping:             Off       On
  Optimization:        Off       On
  Path Detail:        Low   Med  High
  Shape Detail:       Low   Med  High

          Tween       Contour
     +      Create       Cancel
```

Enter the object name **Walls**. Click on **Create** to make the walls.

Go to the 3D Editor by choosing *Program/3D Editor*. The walls have been created in 3D. Right-click on **Zoom Extents** to see the walls in all viewports.

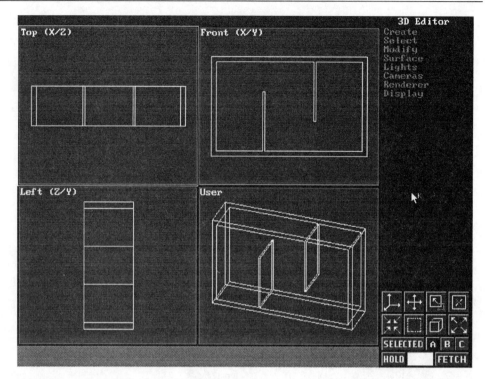

FIGURE 3-16. Walls in 3D Editor.

Save the model as HOUSPLAN.3DS. To do this, choose *File/Save* from the pulldown menus. Enter HOUSPLAN as the filename.

Tutorial 2

In this tutorial you'll draw the following elevation in AutoCAD. This elevation represents a wall with a door and two windows.

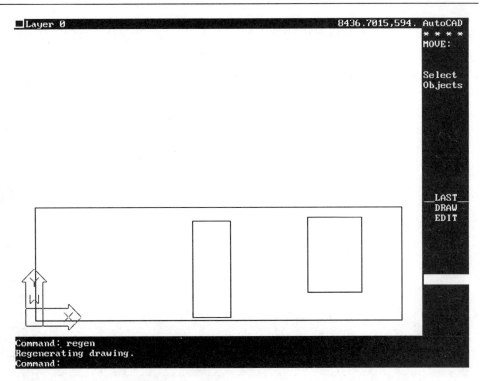

FIGURE 3-17. Wall elevation drawing.

Once the wall is drawn, you'll use the AXROT command to rotate it to the XY plane. The drawing will then be exported to a DXF file and imported to 3D Studio for lofting.

1. Outline

These commands draw a wall section as a closed polyline. The wall is 8000 units long and 2400 units high. It is assumed the lower left corner is at the point 0,0.

> Command: **PLINE**
> From point: **0,0**
> Current line-width is 0.0000
> Arc/Close/Halfwidth/Length/Undo/Width/<Endpoint of line>: **@8000<0**
> Arc/Close/Halfwidth/Length/Undo/Width/<Endpoint of line>: **@2400<90**
> Arc/Close/Halfwidth/Length/Undo/Width/<Endpoint of line>: **@8000<180**
> Arc/Close/Halfwidth/Length/Undo/Width/<Endpoint of line>: **C**

Use the ZOOM command to make the polyline visible on the screen.

> Command: **ZOOM**
> All/Center/Dynamic/Extents/Left/Previous/Vmax/Window/<Scale(X/XP)>:
>   **E**
> Regenerating drawing.
>
> Command: **ZOOM**

All/Center/Dynamic/Extents/Left/Previous/Vmax/Window/<Scale(X/XP)>:
0.9X

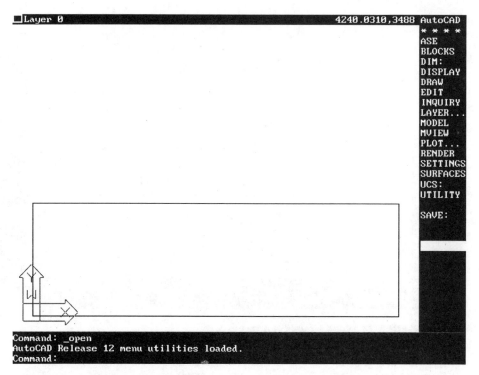

FIGURE 3-18. Wall elevation outline.

2. Door

Next you'll draw a door outline as a closed polyline. The door is 820 units wide and 2050 units high. You will have to pick a point to designate the lower left corner of the door.

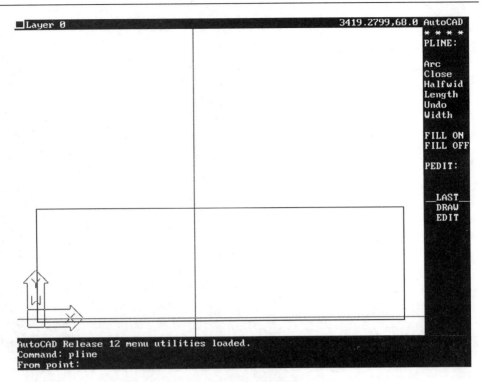

FIGURE 3-19. Point picked for lower left corner of door.

Command: **PLINE**
From point: *(Pick a starting point)*
Current line-width is 0.0000
Arc/Close/Halfwidth/Length/Undo/Width/<Endpoint of line>: **@820<0**
Arc/Close/Halfwidth/Length/Undo/Width/<Endpoint of line>: **@2050<90**
Arc/Close/Halfwidth/Length/Undo/Width/<Endpoint of line>: **@820<180**
Arc/Close/Halfwidth/Length/Undo/Width/<Endpoint of line>: **C**

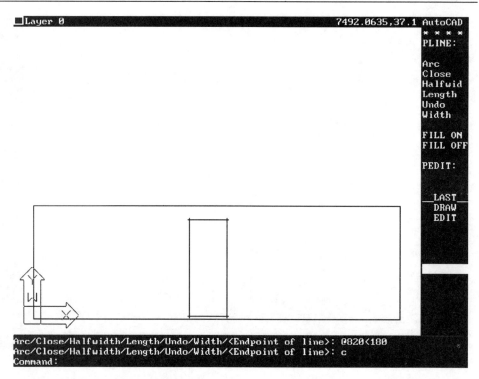

FIGURE 3-20. Wall with door.

3. Window

This command draws a window outline as a closed polyline. The window is 1600 units wide and 1200 units high. You need to pick a point as the lower left corner; the starting point of the polyline outline.

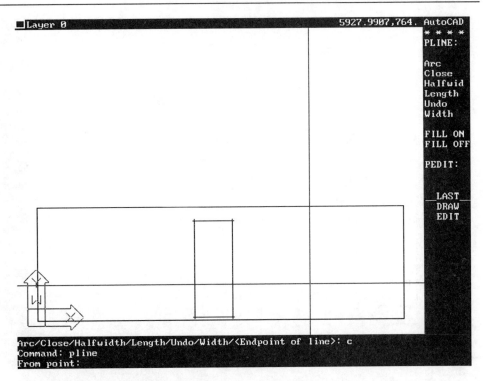

FIGURE 3-21. Pick point for lower left corner of window.

Command: **PLINE**
From point: *(Pick a starting point)*
Current line-width is 0.0000
Arc/Close/Halfwidth/Length/Undo/Width/<Endpoint of line>: **@1200<0**
Arc/Close/Halfwidth/Length/Undo/Width/<Endpoint of line>: **@1600<90**
Arc/Close/Halfwidth/Length/Undo/Width/<Endpoint of line>: **@1200<180**
Arc/Close/Halfwidth/Length/Undo/Width/<Endpoint of line>: **C**

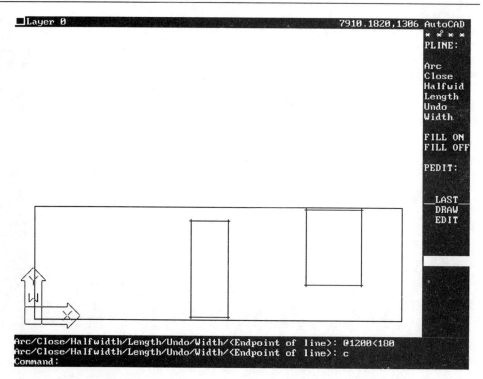

FIGURE 3-22. Wall with window.

Because the elevation was drawn in the XY plane, there is no need to rotate it before exporting it to DXF format.

4. Save the Drawing

> Command: **SAVE**
> Save current changes as: **WALL**
> Current drawing name set to WALL

5. Export to DXF File

The plan can now be output to a DXF file.

> Command: **DXFOUT**
> (Choose the 3D Studio SHAPES directory. Enter the name **WALL**.)
> Enter decimal places of accuracy (0 to 16)/Entities/Binary <6>: **B**

6. Import to 3D Studio

In 3D Studio, go to the 2D Shaper module. To do this, choose the *Program* pulldown menu and choose *2D Shaper*.

Load the DXF file into the 2D Shaper. To do this, choose the *File* pulldown menu and choose *Load*. Click on the *.DXF wildcard field. Locate the subdirectory where WALL.DXF is located. Choose WALL.DXF.

The plan you drew in steps 1 and 2 appears on the screen.

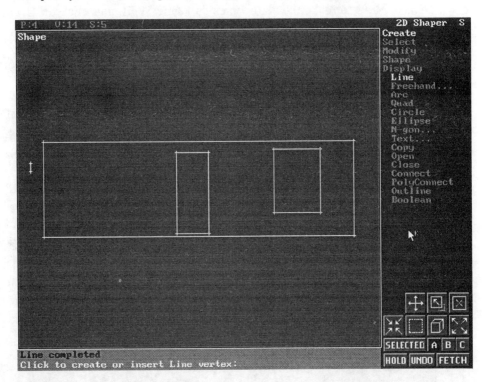

FIGURE 3-23. Wall with window.

7. Draw Path

Next you'll draw a path for the wall elevation. This path will determine the thickness of the wall.

If **Snap** is not on, press the **S** key to turn it on. Choose *Create/Line* and draw a line 250 units long. Watch the top of the screen to see the length of the line as you draw it.

8. Loft Elevation

Choose *Shapes/Assign*. Click on the line you just drew. Go to the 3D Lofter. Bring in the path with *Path/Get/Shaper*. The following message appears:

Click on **OK**.

Go back to the 2D Shaper. Choose *Shapes/Assign/None* to turn off all shapes assignment. Then choose *Shapes/Assign* and click on the wall, door and window polygons.

Go to the 3D Lofter. Choose *Shapes/Get/Shaper* to bring the shapes in. Choose *Objects/Make* to make the wall. Enter the name **Wall**, and click on **Create** to make the wall.

Go to the 3D Editor by choosing *Program/3D Editor*. Right click on Zoom extents. The lofted wall appears on the screen.

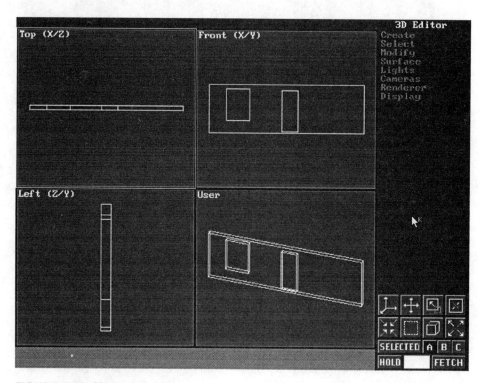

FIGURE 3-24. Wall with window.

9. Save the Model

To save the model, choose *File/Save Project*. Enter the name **WALL**. The file will be saved in 3D Studio file format as **WALL.PRJ**.

EXERCISE

Draw a loftable plan of your own choosing in AutoCAD. Follow the rules stated at the beginning of this chapter for making a loftable plan. Export the plan to a DXF file and import it to 3D Studio. Draw a lofting path of suitable length and use it to loft the plan into a 3D model. Look at the model in the 3D Editor.

4

3D DRAWING
IN AUTOCAD

One way to make an AutoCAD 3D drawing for rendering is to complete the drawing in AutoCAD. The drawing can then be exported to 3D Studio via a DXF file. The advantages of this method are:

• AutoCAD is more accurate than 3D Studio. Any extra accuracy is lost in the conversion to 3D Studio, but many users find AutoCAD's accuracy helpful during the drawing process.

• If you're more familiar with AutoCAD than 3D Studio, your drawing will be faster and easier.

• Most drawing processes can be performed in either AutoCAD or 3D Studio, but certain procedures are much easier in AutoCAD. As you learn each package you'll develop a sense of what should be drawn where.

In this chapter you'll learn about AutoCAD commands that can be used to produce a 3D drawing. At the end of the chapter is a tutorial for creating a simple house drawing.

3D CONCEPTS

The creation of 3D entities in AutoCAD requires the use of specific commands. To make a 3D drawing, you might be tempted to simply draw LINEs representing the three-dimensional wireframe of your drawing. Unfortunately, this type of drawing is not considered to be a "true" 3D drawing. When you export such a drawing to DXF format then import it to 3D Studio, some or all of the model will be missing.

For the purpose of this book, any 2D or 3D item made in AutoCAD will be called an *entity*. When the AutoCAD drawing is exported to 3D Studio, the entities are converted to 3D *objects*. Within AutoCAD, the term *object* is used to describe any entity you've drawn on the screen, whether it's 2D or 3D. For example, AutoCAD sometimes asks you to pick an "object" from the screen. In this book, however, the term *object* refers to 3D Studio objects only. All items drawn in AutoCAD will be referred to as *entities*.

In order to make a drawing that can be exported to 3D Studio, each part of the drawing must be created as a "true" 3D entity. By this we mean entities that are recognized by 3D Studio as having 3D solidity. The commands for creating "true" 3D entities are discussed in the section that follows. Once you become familiar with the commands that will do the job, it's a matter of working out which commands will work best for each part of your drawing.

Several AutoCAD entities can be made to form one 3D Studio object as long as all the related entities reside on one layer. When the AutoCAD drawing is exported to 3D Studio, the conversion process takes all the entities on one layer and glues them together to form a single 3D Studio object. Each layer forms a separate 3D Studio object.

There are many ways to create 3D entities in AutoCAD. Methods of creating 3D entities in AutoCAD can be broken down into four distinct types:

- *Extrusion*, where a 2D entity is given a Z thickness to create a 3D entity;
- *Surfacing*, which creates a 3D surface from two or more 2D entities;
- *Solid Modeling,* which creates solid entities such as cubes, cylinders and spheres, and uses them to construct more complex entities; and
- The *3D Face* method, where a set of specified points define a 3D face.

The methods are listed roughly in order of complexity. For rectangular entities such as doors, the *Extrusion* method is sufficient. For contoured entities such as dome ceilings and rounded walls, the *Surfacing* method must be used. *Solid Modeling* can be used to make many types of solid entities such as walls with windows.

Sometimes the methods can be combined. For example, extruded entities may be used to define some surfaced entities.

At times, none of the first three methods will suffice. In these cases you'll have to draw individual 3D faces in AutoCAD, or build the parts of the model in 3D Studio. It is recommended that you avoid making 3D faces in AutoCAD when you first start working in 3D. Building individual 3D faces is more prone to error than the first two methods.

EXTRUSION METHOD

A 3D entity has "height" (or "tallness") on the Z axis. In AutoCAD, this height is called *thickness*. AutoCAD has commands for setting or changing the thickness value (height) of an entity. In some cases, setting a thickness value greater than zero will cause a 2D entity to extrude into a 3D entity.

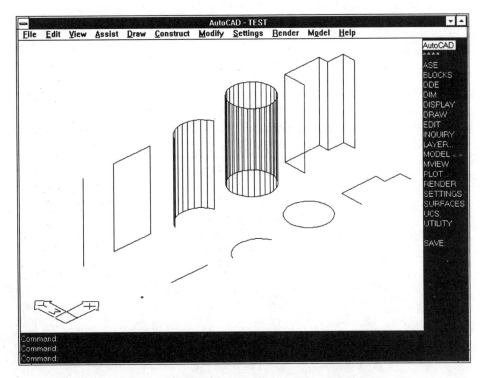

FIGURE 4-1. Entities with thickness, and at various elevations.

The term *elevation* refers to the location of an entity on the Z plane. With 3D entities, the elevation is the height of the base of the entity. In general, the elevation determines where the "bottom" of the entity sits on the Z plane.

Commands

In AutoCAD, several commands can be used to draw an entity with an elevation and thickness. These commands are listed in Figure 4-2.

ARC	3D arc
CIRCLE	Cylinder
SOLID	Rectangular prism
TEXT	3D text
TRACE	Rectangular prism
PLINE	One or more faces
LINE	3D face

FIGURE 4-2. Commands that can be used to produce true 3D entities with thickness and elevation.

The SOLID and TRACE commands date back to several versions of AutoCAD. In practice they have been replaced by PLINE which offers more flexibility.

In order to create true 3D entities, the thickness and elevation must be set with the CHPROP, CHANGE or ELEV commands.

CHPROP

The CHPROP command can be used in conjunction with the commands in Table 4-2 to produce 3D entities. To use CHPROP with these commands, you first draw a 2D entity with one of the commands in Table 4-2. You can then use CHPROP to change the thickness which will extrude the 2D entity into a 3D entity.

Command: **CHPROP**
Select object: *(Pick object to be extruded.)*
Properties/<Change point>: **P** ⬅
Change what property (Color/LAyer/LType/Thickness)?: **T**
New thickness <0.0000>: **2500**

In the example above, the thickness has been set to 2500 units. A negative thickness may also be entered to make the entity extrude downward from the elevation.

As an example we'll use the CIRCLE command from Table 4-2 with the CHPROP command. This will produce a 3D cylinder.

Command: **CIRCLE**
3P/2P/TTR/<Center point>: *(Pick a point on the screen.)*
Diameter/<Radius>: **500**

Command: **ZOOM**
All/Center/Dynamic/Extents/Left/Previous/Vmax/Window/<Scale(X/XP)>: **E**
Regenerating drawing.

Change the viewpoint with the VPOINT command.

Command: **VPOINT**
Rotate/<View point> <0.0000,0.0000,1.0000>: **1,1,1**

If necessary, use the ZOOM command to see the circle on the screen.

Command: **ZOOM**
All/Center/Dynamic/Extents/Left/Previous/Vmax/Window/<Scale(X/XP)>: **0.8X**
Regenerating drawing.

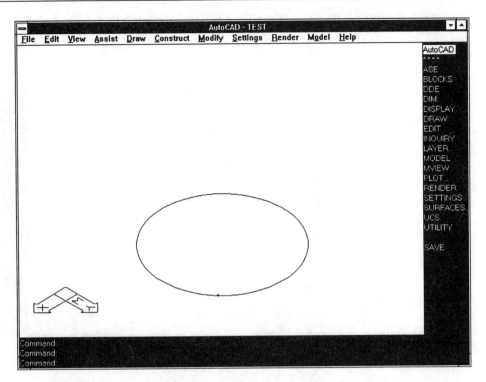

FIGURE 4- 3. A circle with radius 500.

Next you'll use CHPROP to give the circle a thickness.

> Command: **CHPROP**
> Select object: *(Pick entity to be extruded.)*
> Select object:
> Change what property (Color/LAyer/LType/Thickness) ? **T**
> New thickness <0.0000>: **2000**
> Change what property (Color/LAyer/LType/Thickness) ?

The circle has been extruded to a cylinder with a thickness (height) of 2000 units.

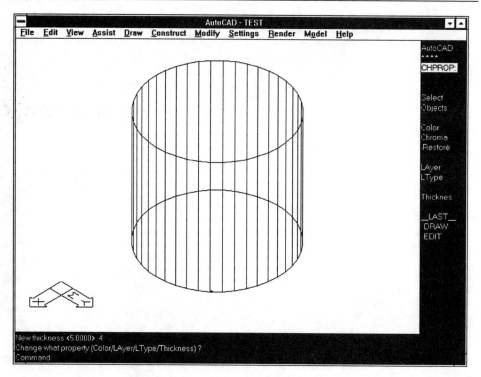

FIGURE 4-4. A cylinder.

CHANGE

The CHANGE command can be also be used with the commands in Table 4-2. CHANGE can be used to change both the thickness and elevation of the entity.

To use CHANGE, first draw a 2D entity with one of the commands in Table 4-2, then use CHANGE to extrude the 2D entity into a 3D entity. You can also use CHANGE to change the elevation.

> Command: **CHANGE**
> Select object: *(Pick entity to be extruded.)*
> Properties/<Change point>: **P** ⟵⎯
> Change what property (Color/Elev/LAyer/LType/Thickness)?:

Entering **E** at the prompt will change the elevation, while entering **T** will change the thickness. After entering **E** or **T**, enter the new elevation or thickness value.

As an example, use PLINE with the CHANGE command to produce a 3D entity. First use VPOINT to change to an angled view of the drawing.

> Command: **VPOINT**
> Rotate/<View point> <0.0000,0.0000,1.0000>: **1,0.5,1**
>
> Command: **PLINE**

From point: **-1800,600**
Current line-width is 0.0000
Arc/Close/Halfwidth/Length/Undo/Width/<Endpoint of line>: **-1300,600**
Arc/Close/Halfwidth/Length/Undo/Width/<Endpoint of line>: **-1300,1100**
Arc/Close/Halfwidth/Length/Undo/Width/<Endpoint of line>: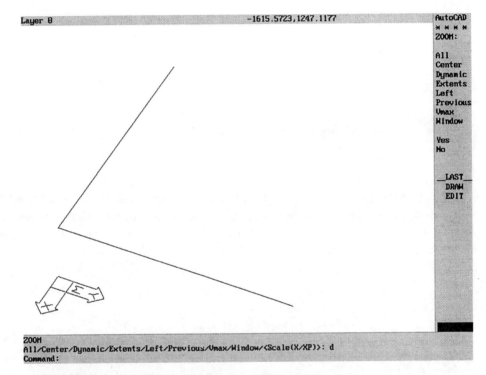

Command: **ZOOM**
All/Center/Dynamic/Extents/Left/Previous/Vmax/Window/<Scale(X/XP)>: **E**
Regenerating drawing.

A PLINE appears on the screen.

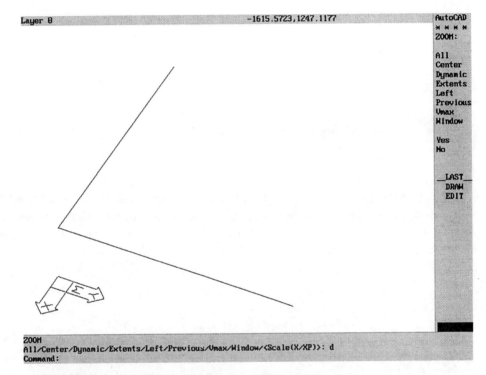

FIGURE 4-5. A PLINE to receive elevation and thickness.

Command: **CHANGE**
Select object: *(Pick PLINE object just created.)*
Properties/<Change point>: **P**
Change what property (Color/Elev/LAyer/LType/Thickness)?: **E**
New elevation <0.0000> **200**
Change what property (Color/Elev/LAyer/LType/Thickness)?: **T**
New thickness <0.0000>: **250**
Change what property (Color/Elev/LAyer/LType/Thickness)?:

A 3D entity, much like the corner of a room, has been created.

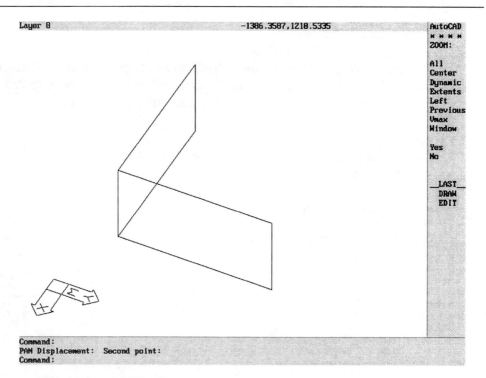

FIGURE 4-6. PLINE with thickness and elevation.

In some versions of AutoCAD the CHANGE command cannot be used to adjust the elevation. If the *Elev* option is not displayed as a property when you use the CHANGE command, then your version of AutoCAD does not support it. In this case, use the ELEV command to change the elevation.

ELEV

The ELEV command can also be used in conjunction with the commands in Table 4-2 to produce true 3D entities. The ELEV command is used before using the commands in Table 4-2 to specify the current elevation and thickness for subsequently drawn entities.

> Command: **ELEV**
> New current elevation <current>: **100**
> New current thickness <current>: **250**

Once the ELEV command has been used to set the elevation and extrusion thickness, any 2D entity drawn with the commands in Table 4-2 will become a 3D entity. Use the ELEV command before using the drawing command.

In this example you'll create a rectangular prism with the SOLID command. Use VPOINT first to change to an angled view if necessary.

> Command: **VPOINT**
> Rotate/<View point> <0.0000,0.0000,1.0000>: **1,0.5,1**

Use the ELEV command to change the elevation and thickness before drawing the entity.

Command: **ELEV**
New current elevation <0.0>: **200**
New current thickness <0.0>: **250**

Command: **SOLID**
First point: **-3000,1400**
Second point: **-2500,1400**
Third point: **-3000,1900**
Fourth point: **-2500,1900**
Third point: ⬅

A box appears on the screen.

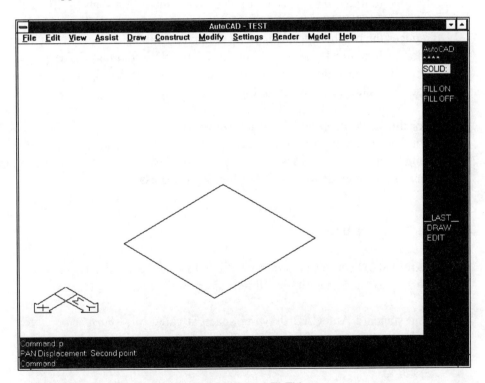

FIGURE 4-7. Box created with SOLID and ELEV.

The SOLID command has, for the most part, been replaced by the PLINE command. However, it can be used to quickly create basic 3D shapes, such as the box above.

Command Summary

The CHPROP, CHANGE, and ELEV commands can be used with the commands in Table 4-2 to produce 3D entities. Table 4-8 shows how these commands are used.

	Thickness	Elevation	Usage
CHPROP	yes	no	After drawing command
CHANGE	yes	yes	After drawing command
ELEV	yes	yes	Before drawing command

FIGURE 4-8. How 3D Commands are used.

PLINE

In AutoCAD, lines can be drawn with either the LINE or PLINE commands. It's more flexible to draw lines with the PLINE command rather than LINE. A PLINE (a polyline drawn with PLINE) of several segments can be moved or edited as a single entity, which reduces the number of screen picks you have to make. A PLINE can always be converted back to individual lines by using the EXPLODE command. The points along a PLINE will always have the same Z coordinate (height) as the polyline's starting point, which is not always the case with an ordinary LINE.

For this book, the term 3D PLINE refers to a polyline with a thickness. A 2D PLINE is a polyline drawn with no thickness. A 2D PLINE may have X, Y and Z coordinates, as long as it has no thickness. The term PLINE without a 2D or 3D designation refers to any PLINE regardless of whether it has a thickness.

UCS and WCS

Extruded 3D entities are always extruded along the Z axis. There will be times when you wish to extrude an entity in a direction other than the default Z axis.

The standard AutoCAD drawing space is called the *World Coordinate System (WCS)*. This is the master reference for all 3D geometry. Within this reference system you can define one or more custom reference systems which may be more suited to your current 3D task.

This custom reference system is called the *User Coordinate System (UCS)*. You can define many UCSs but only one may be current at any time. The UCS defaults to the WCS at first. When you make a new UCS with the X,Y coordinates in a direction different from the WCS, the orientation of the Z axis changes accordingly. If you make this new UCS the current UCS and use the CHPROP, CHANGE or ELEV commands, the 3D entity will be extruded along the new Z axis.

To make a new UCS, use the UCS command.

> Command: **UCS**
> Origin/ZAxis/3point/Entity/View/X/Y/Z/Prev/Restore/Save/Del/<World>:

In general, the first half of the UCS command options are used to define the UCS. The last half are used for maintenance tasks such as saving, deleting and resetting the UCS. The most commonly used options are:

Origin. Set the origin point for the UCS. If you enter only X, Y coordinates, the Z coordinate is assumed to be the current elevation.

Zaxis. Used to define a new UCS with the origin point and a point along the Z axis.

3point. Asks for three points: the origin, one point on the X axis and one on the Y.

Restore. Makes a previously saved UCS the current UCS.

Save. Names and saves the UCS.

World. Resets the UCS to the WCS.

In practice, you would use the Origin, Zaxis or 3point options to set up a UCS, then name it with the Save option. You could then use the UCS at any time with the Restore option.

In this book all drawing is accomplished without changing the UCS. When you become more proficient with 3D you may want to experiment with the UCS as it can make some drawing operations easier.

SURFACING METHOD

The Surfacing method is the best way to make smooth or complex entities. These entities are made with one of several surfacing commands.

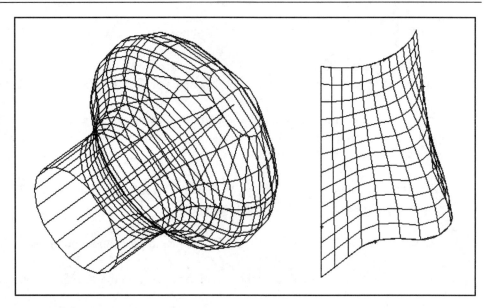

FIGURE 4-9. Surfaced entities.

With surfacing commands, two or more LINEs or PLINEs are drawn first to help define the surface. After the 3D entity is drawn, the LINEs and PLINEs used to define it remain on the screen. They can be deleted with the ERASE command if desired.

REVSURF

The REVSURF command rotates an entity around an axis of revolution to create a curved 3D entity. REVSURF is useful for creating rounded surfaces such as domed ceilings, ornate furniture legs and balusters.

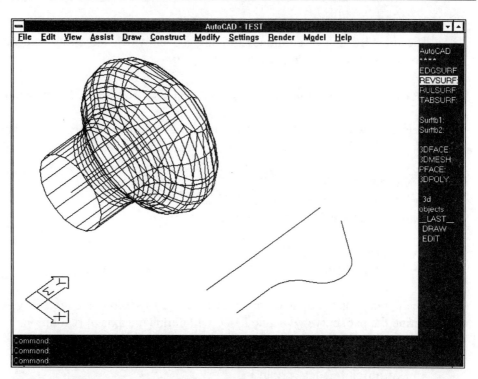

FIGURE 4-10. Lines to define REVSURFed entity, and REVSURFed entity.

To use REVSURF you need two entities: one to define the shape of the outer edge of the entity, and one to define the axis of rotation.

Command: **REVSURF**
Select path curve: *(Select an entity)*
Select axis of rotation: *(Select an entity)*
Start angle <0>: *(Enter an angle value)*
Included angle (+=ccw,-=cw) <Full circle>: *(Enter an angle value)*

The path curve defines the shape of the surface edge (the "profile"). It can be any one of the following entities:

LINE
ARC
CIRCLE
2D PLINE
3D PLINE

The axis of rotation is defined by the LINE or 2D PLINE describing the axis of revolution. This line defines an axis in space, and the path curve is rotated about this axis to form a surface. The entity is created and placed around the rotation axis.

The start angle determines the angle at which the rotation will start. Most entities you create will be closed. In this case the start angle is not important, and the default value of zero can be used.

The included angle determines the angle over which the entity will be rotated. For a closed entity, choose Full circle.

As an example, the following command sequence draws the 3D entity in Figure 4-11.

Before drawing the entities, set the thickness and elevation variables back to zero, and use the VPOINT command to set the viewpoint to 1,-1,1:

```
Command: ELEV
New Current Elevation<200.0000>: 0
New Current Thickness<250.0000>: 0

Command: VPOINT
Rotate/<Viewpoint> <0.0000, 0.0000, 1.0000>: 1,-1,1
```

The commands below will draw a PLINE and LINE to make the entity. The PLINE will define the path curve while the LINE will define the axis of revolution.

```
Command: PLINE
From point: (Pick a point)
Current line-width is 0.0000
Arc/Close/Halfwidth/Length/Undo/Width/<Endpoint of line>: @100<90
Arc/Close/Halfwidth/Length/Undo/Width/<Endpoint of line>: A
Angle/CEnter/CLose/Direction/Halfwidth/Line/Radius/Second pt/Undo/Width/
<Endpoint of arc>: @100<45
Angle/CEnter/CLose/Direction/Halfwidth/Line/Radius/Second pt/Undo/Width/
<Endpoint of arc>: A
Included angle: 135
Angle/CEnter/CLose/Direction/Halfwidth/Line/Radius/Second pt/Undo/Width/
<Endpoint of arc>: @100<60
Angle/CEnter/CLose/Direction/Halfwidth/Line/Radius/Second pt/Undo/Width/
<Endpoint of arc>: L
Arc/Close/Halfwidth/Length/Undo/Width/<Endpoint of line>: @150<120
Arc/Close/Halfwidth/Length/Undo/Width/<Endpoint of line>: ⏎

Command: LINE
From point: (pick a point slightly to the left of the above curve)
To point: @400<90
To point: ⏎
```

The SURFTAB1 variable sets the smoothness of the curved surface. A SURFTAB1 value of 6 will not define a smooth curve. Change the value to 12 for a smoother entity.

```
Command: SURFTAB1
New value for SURFTAB1 <6>: 12
```

The SURFTAB1 variable is covered in the *Surfacing Variables* section later in this chapter.

> Command: **REVSURF**
> Select path curve: *(Pick the PLINE)*
> Select axis of revolution: *(Pick the LINE)*
> Start angle <0>: ⟵⎯⎯⎤
> Included angle (+=ccw, -=cw) <Full circle>: ⟵⎯⎯⎤

RULESURF

The RULESURF command creates a 3D surface connecting two curves.
It can be used to make door frames, roof cornices, baseboards and architraves.

> Command: **RULESURF**
> Select first defining curve: *(Pick an entity)*
> Select second defining curve: *(Pick an entity)*

The defining curves can be any one of the following entities:

> LINE
> POINT
> ARC
> CIRCLE
> 2D PLINE
> 3D PLINE

Only one entity can be POINT, not both.

As an example we will use a LINE and a PLINE to define the RULESURF surface. The PLINE is the same one used for the REVSURF surface. If you have already drawn this PLINE in the previous example, you can use it here rather than drawing it again.

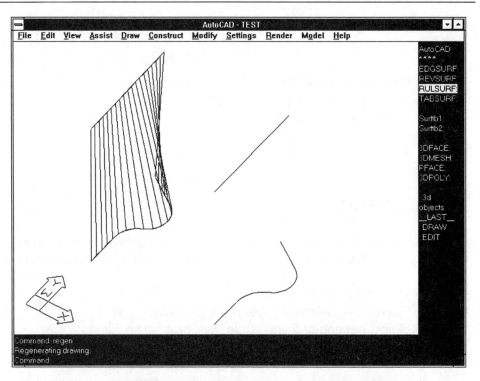

FIGURE 4-11. RULESURF defining entities and resulting 3D entity.

Command: **PLINE**
From point: *(Pick a point)*
Current line-width is 0.0000
Arc/Close/Halfwidth/Length/Undo/Width/<Endpoint of line>: **@100<90**
Arc/Close/Halfwidth/Length/Undo/Width/<Endpoint of line>: **A**
Angle/CEnter/CLose/Direction/Halfwidth/Line/Radius/Second pt/Undo/Width/
<Endpoint of arc>: **@100<45**
Angle/CEnter/CLose/Direction/Halfwidth/Line/Radius/Second pt/Undo/Width/
<Endpoint of arc>: **A**
Included angle: **135**
Angle/CEnter/CLose/Direction/Halfwidth/Line/Radius/Second pt/Undo/Width/
<Endpoint of arc>: **@100<60**
Angle/CEnter/CLose/Direction/Halfwidth/Line/Radius/Second pt/Undo/Width/
<Endpoint of arc>: **L**
Arc/Close/Halfwidth/Length/Undo/Width/<Endpoint of line>: **@150<120**
Arc/Close/Halfwidth/Length/Undo/Width/<Endpoint of line>: ⬅

Next you'll draw a LINE and raise it along the Z axis by 500 units.

Command: **LINE**
From point: **ENDP** *(Pick lower end of PLINE)*
To point: **@400<90**
To point: ⬅

Command: **MOVE**

Select objects: *(Pick LINE just drawn)*
1 found
Select objects: ⟨◄─────⟩
Base point or displacement: *(Pick any point on screen)*
Second point of displacement: **@0,0,500**

Command: **RULESURF**
Select first defining curve: *(Pick the PLINE)*
Select second defining curve: *(Pick the LINE)*

You may see the resulting mesh twisted in a way known as "hourglassing". Hourglassing occurs frequently in objects made with the RULESURF command. The way to prevent hourglassing is to pick points near the same end of the two defining entities. If your RULESURF command resulted in an hourglass, type U to undo and R to redraw, and perform the rulesurf again:

Command: **RULESURF**
Select first defining curve: (pick near one end of the pline)
Select second defining curve: (pick near same end of the line)

Now the mesh should appear correct.

TABSURF

The TABSURF command sends one entity along a vector defined by another entity. The start and end points of the second entity are used to define the direction vector. TABSURF performs a simple extrusion, but with the advantage that the direction of extrusion is not limited to the Z axis.

TABSURF can be used to create a shaped edge around a tabletop or picture frame.

Command: **TABSURF**
Select path curve: *(Pick an entity)*
Select direction vector: *(Pick an entity)*

The *path curve* is the entity to be sent along the direction vector. The path curve can be any one of the following entities:

LINE
ARC
CIRCLE
2D PLINE
3D PLINE

The direction vector can be any one of the following:

LINE
2D PLINE
3D PLINE

The TABSURF command uses the start and end points of the LINE or PLINE to determine the direction vector.

In this example you'll make a curved surface with TABSURF.

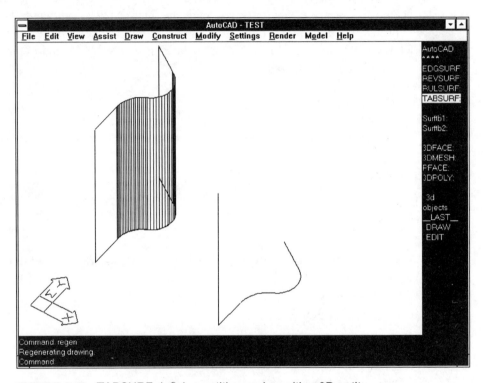

FIGURE 4-12. TABSURF defining entities and resulting 3D entity.

This example uses the same PLINE once again.

```
Command: PLINE
From point: (Pick a point)
Current line-width is 0.0000
Arc/Close/Halfwidth/Length/Undo/Width/<Endpoint of line>: @100<90
Arc/Close/Halfwidth/Length/Undo/Width/<Endpoint of line>: A
Angle/CEnter/CLose/Direction/Halfwidth/Line/Radius/Second
pt/Undo/Width/
<Endpoint of arc>: @100<45
Angle/CEnter/CLose/Direction/Halfwidth/Line/Radius/Second
pt/Undo/Width/
<Endpoint of arc>: A
```

Included angle: **135**
Angle/CEnter/CLose/Direction/Halfwidth/Line/Radius/Second
pt/Undo/Width/
<Endpoint of arc>: **@100<60**
Angle/CEnter/CLose/Direction/Halfwidth/Line/Radius/Second
pt/Undo/Width/
<Endpoint of arc>: **L**
Arc/Close/Halfwidth/Length/Undo/Width/<Endpoint of line>: **@150<120**
Arc/Close/Halfwidth/Length/Undo/Width/<Endpoint of line>: ⏎

Next, a LINE is drawn from the endpoint of the PLINE. The LINE does not need to be attached to the PLINE, but drawing the entities this way makes the TABSURF entity easier to visualize.

Command: **LINE**
From point: **ENDP** *(Pick either end of the PLINE)*
To point: **@0,0,500**
To point: ⏎

Command: **TABSURF**
Select path curve: *(Pick the PLINE)*
Select direction vector: *(Pick the LINE)*

In the same way pick points affected how RULESURF worked, and they also affect how TABSURF works. To illustrate this point, perform the TABSURF twice, first picking from the lower end of the direction vector (the line), and the second time picking from the upper end of the line. When you pick the upper end of the line, you should see that the mesh created below the path curve (the pline) is exactly the opposite of the expected result. Picking on the end of the direction vector closest to the path curve will give predictable results.

EDGESURF

The EDGESURF command creates a surface from four curved entities. It can be used to create various types of surfaces. EDGESURF is suited to making irregular surface shapes such as molded plastic or fiberglass.

Command: **EDGESURF**
Select edge 1: *(Select an edge)*
Select edge 2: *(Select an edge)*
Select edge 3: *(Select an edge)*
Select edge 4: *(Select an edge)*

The edges can be any one of the following entities:

LINE
ARC
2D PLINE
3D PLINE

The four curved edges must touch at the endpoints. A problem results with EDGESURF when the ends of any one of the four edges do not exactly connect with the adjacent edge. The mismatch may be tiny, but EDGESURF needs a perfect join. This problem most often occurs when an inherently 2D object such as an ARC or 2D PLINE is used on adjacent edges. 3D PLINEs are inherently 3D in nature and will always join exactly provided OSNAP is used.

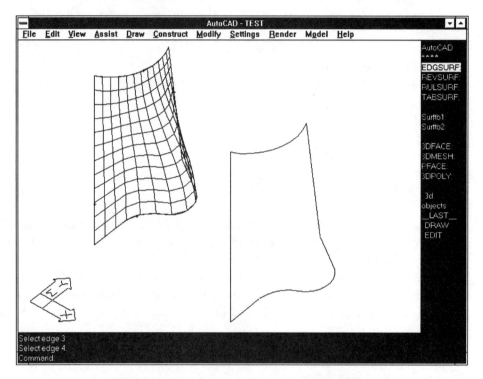

FIGURE 4-13. EDGESURF defining entities and resulting 3D entity.

In this example you'll use four entities to create a surface patch with EDGESURF. To ensure that the ends of the four sides meet, we will use more complex entities such as PLINE and ARC for two of the sides, and a LINE for the other two sides. OSNAP will also be used to make sure the curved edges touch at the endpoints.

The PLINE drawn earlier will be used as one side of a surface patch. If you have already drawn this PLINE, you need not draw it again.

Command: **PLINE**
From point: *(Pick a point)*
Current line-width is 0.0000
Arc/Close/Halfwidth/Length/Undo/Width/<Endpoint of line>: **@100<90**
Arc/Close/Halfwidth/Length/Undo/Width/<Endpoint of line>: **A**

Angle/CEnter/CLose/Direction/Halfwidth/Line/Radius/Second pt/Undo/Width/
<Endpoint of arc>: **@100<45**
Angle/CEnter/CLose/Direction/Halfwidth/Line/Radius/Second pt/Undo/Width/
<Endpoint of arc>: **A**
Included angle: **135**
Angle/CEnter/CLose/Direction/Halfwidth/Line/Radius/Second pt/Undo/Width/
<Endpoint of arc>: **@100<60**
Angle/CEnter/CLose/Direction/Halfwidth/Line/Radius/Second pt/Undo/Width/
<Endpoint of arc>: **L**
Arc/Close/Halfwidth/Length/Undo/Width/<Endpoint of line>: **@150<120**
Arc/Close/Halfwidth/Length/Undo/Width/<Endpoint of line>: ⟵

Draw an ARC and move it 500 units along the Z axis.

Command: **ARC**
Center/<Start point>: *(Pick a point)*
Center/End/<Second point>: *(Pick another point)*
End point: *(Pick a third point to drag arc to shape)*

Command: **MOVE**
Select objects: *(Pick the ARC)*
1 found
Select objects: ⟵
Base point or displacement: *(Pick any point on the screen)*
Second point of displacement: **@0,0,500**

Attach the ends of the PLINE and ARC with lines, using OSNAP to make sure they join accurately.

Command: **OSNAP**
Object snap modes: **ENDP**

Command: **LINE**
From point: *(Pick one end of PLINE)*
To point: *(Pick equivalent end of ARC)*
To point: ⟵

Command: **LINE**
From point: *(Pick other end of PLINE)*
To point: *(Pick other end of ARC)*
To point: ⟵

Now use the EDGESURF command to create the surface.

Command: **EDGESURF**
Select edge 1: *(Pick the PLINE)*
Select edge 2: *(Pick the adjoining LINE)*

Select edge 3: *(Pick the ARC)*
Select edge 4: *(Pick the remaining LINE)*

EDGESURF is the most flexible of the surfacing commands, but can also be the most complex.

Surfacing Variables

The smoothness of a surfaced entity depends on how many vertices the entity has. The number of vertices is determined by the SURFTAB1 and SURFTAB2 variables.

These variables affect the surfacing commands as follows.

	SURFTAB1	**SURFTAB2**
REVSURF	Around the circle	Down the length
RULESURF	Across surface	(no effect)
TABSURF	Along the direction vector	(no effect)
EDGESURF	Along one direction	Along the other direction

FIGURE 4-14. Surfacing variables and their effects on surfacing commands.

For example, suppose the variable SURFTAB1 is set to 12 and SURFTAB2 is set to 6. When you use the REVSURF command, the entity will be created with 12 sections around and 6 sections along the length of the entity.

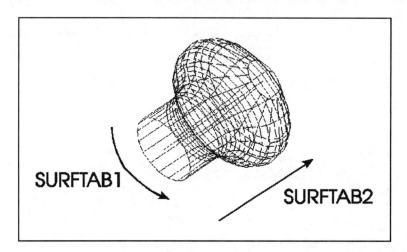

FIGURE 4-15. How SURFTAB variables affect the detail on a REVSURFed entity.

SURFTAB1 and SURFTAB2 always default to a value of 6. They can be set using the SETVAR command.

Command: **SETVAR**
Variable name or ?: **SURFTAB1**
New value for SURFTAB1 <6>: **24**

You can also use the variable names to set the variable values.

> Command: **SURFTAB1**
> New value for SURFTAB1 <6>: **24**

As a rough guide you can assume one SURFTAB increment per 10 degrees of surface curvature. For example, to create an entity with REVSURF which revolves over 360 degrees, a SURFTAB1 value of 36 would provide sufficient detail for most drawings. 3D Studio automatically applies 10 degrees of surface curvature when importing extruded arcs and circles from AutoCAD.

With the EDGESURF command, the application of the SURFTAB1 and SURFTAB2 values depends on which edge is picked first. If you have widely different values for the two variables and your EDGESURF entity comes out wrong, just UNDO and start again. This time, pick the entity adjacent to the one you picked previously.

The more vertices an entity has the smoother it will appear in 3D renderings. However, too many vertices make an entity difficult to work with and will increase rendering time. After some practice with 3D entities you will be able to determine the minimum number of vertices necessary to get the detail you want in your renderings.

SOLID MODELING

With solid modeling, you can individual make solid objects such as those shown below. These solid objects are called *primitives*.

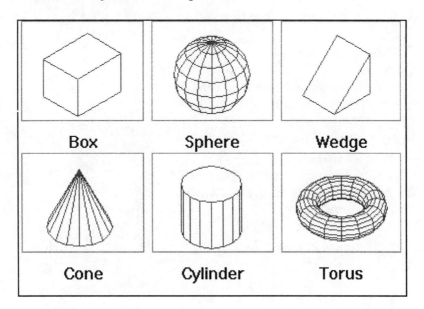

FIGURE 4-16. 3D primitives.

You can also combine primitives to make more complex objects. To make a sphere with a hole in it, for example, you can subtract a cylinder from a sphere.

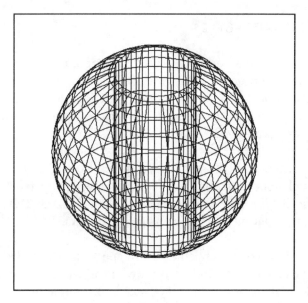

FIGURE 4-17. Complex object made from primitives.

Primitives

Primitives are created with commands beginning with the letters SOL.

Box. The sides of each box can have different lengths, or the box can be a cube.

```
Command: SOLBOX
Corner of box: (Enter corner point of box.)
Cube/Length/<Other corner>: LENGTH
Length: (Enter a length.)
Width: (Enter a width.)
Height: (Enter a height.)
Command: SOLBOX
Corner of box: (Enter corner point of box.)
Cube/Length/<Other corner>: CUBE
Length: (Enter a length.)
```

Sphere. A sphere is created by entering the center point and radius or diameter of the sphere.

```
Command: SOLSPHERE
Baseline/<Center of sphere>: (Enter a point.)
Diameter/<Radius of sphere>: (Enter a radius.)
```

Wedge. A wedge is constructed by specifying the dimensions of the base, then the height of the end of the wedge.

Command: **SOLWEDGE**
Baseline//<Corner of wedge>: *(Enter a point.)*
Length/<Other corner>: *(Enter a point.)*
Height: *(Enter a point.)*

Cone. A cone can be constructed with either a circular or elliptical base. Its base will lie in the current X/Y plane. The size of the base and the height are specified to construct the cone.

Command:**SOLCONE**
Baseline/Elliptical/<Center point>: *(Enter a point.)*
Diameter/<Radius>: *(Enter a radius.)*
Apex/<Height>: *(Enter a height.)*

To create a cone with an elliptical base, follow a command sequence similar to the one used to make an ellipse. See Figure 4-18 for the points referenced in the command sequence.

Command: **SOLCONE**
Baseline/Elliptical/<Center point>: **ELLIPTICAL**
<Axis endpoint 1>/Center: *(Enter first axis endpoint.)*
Axis endpoint 2: *(Enter second axis endpoint.)*
Other axis distance: *(Enter third axis endpoint.)*
Apex/<Height>:*(Enter a height.)*

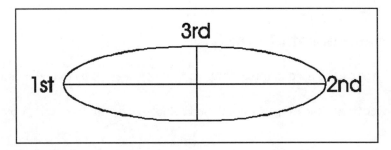

FIGURE 4-18. Ellipse entry points.

Cylinder. Like a cone, a cylinder can be constructed with a circular or elliptical base.

Command: **SOLCYL**
Baseline/Elliptical/<Center point>: *(Enter a point.)*
Diameter/<Radius>: *(Enter a radius.)*
Center of other end/<Height>: *(Enter a height.)*

To enter a cylinder with an elliptical base, enter ELLIPSE and follow the instructions above for SOLCONE.

Torus. A torus is a round tube, like a donut. A torus is constructed by entering the radius or diameter for the torus and the tube. Figure 4-19 illustrates the components of a torus.

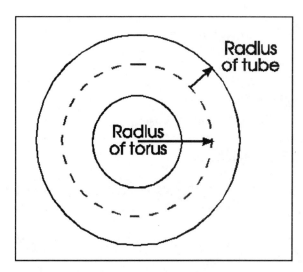

FIGURE 4-19. Radius of torus and tube.

Command: **SOLTORUS**
Baseline/<Center of torus>: *(Enter a point.)*
Diameter/<Radius> of torus: *(Enter a radius.)*
Diameter/<Radius> of tube: *(Enter a radius.)*

Operations with Primitives

Primitives can be used in three different types of operations to make other solid objects.

Intersection. The SOLINT command calculates the intersection of two primitives.

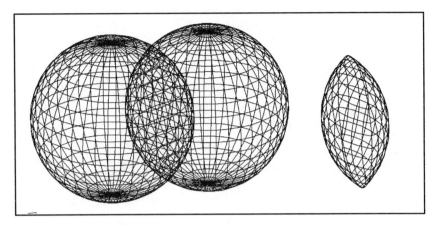

FIGURE 4-20. Intersection of two spheres.

Command: **SOLINT**
Select objects: *(Pick two objects for intersection.)*

Subtraction. The SOLSUB command subtracts one primitive from another.

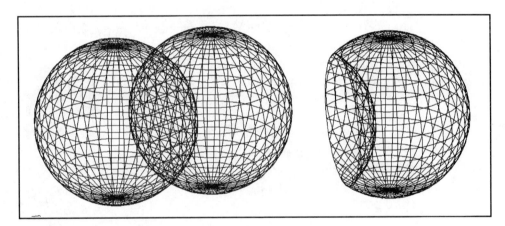

FIGURE 4-21. Subtraction with two spheres.

Command: **SOLSUB**
Source objects...
Select objects: *(Pick objects to subtract from.)*
Objects to subtract from them...
Select objects: *(Pick objects to subtract.)*

Union. The SOLUNION command joins two primitives together as a single entity. If the primitives overlap, SOLUNION erases all redundant vertices.

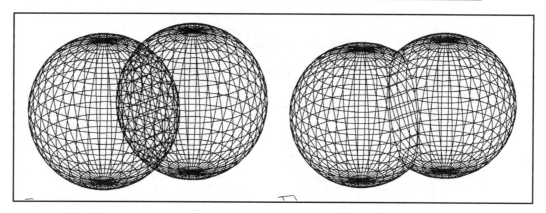

FIGURE 4-22. Union of two spheres.

Command: **SOLUNION**
Select objects: *(Pick objects to join together.)*

3D FACE METHOD

An entity created with the 3DFACE command is simply a 3 or 4 sided facet which defines a surface. Occasionally you may find that one of your 3D entities is impossible to create with the Extrusion, Surfacing or Solid Modeling methods. In this case the entity will have to be built by drawing individual 3D faces with the 3DFACE command.

Command: **3DFACE**
First point: *(Pick a point)*
Second point: *(Pick a point)*
Third point: *(Pick a point)*
Fourth point: *(Pick a point)*
Third point: ⬅️

The points defining the corners of the face can be placed anywhere in 3D space. A triangular element is created by responding with the ⬅️ key when asked for the fourth point. To create a four-sided face, enter a fourth point.

You can continue to enter points to create a series of adjacent 3D faces. The second time the third point is requested, the 3DFACE command assumes you'd like to create another 3D face using the third and fourth points of the previous entry as the first and second points for the face. In this way, several 3D faces can be made in succession.

In using the 3DFACE command you must take care to select the correct points. One way to approach this is to create 2D PLINEs and use them as snap points while drawing the 3D face.

If you have to use the 3DFACE command, it's a good idea to draw all your faces in a consistently in the same direction. For example, you might draw all faces starting from the top left corner and working clockwise. The method you use is not important -- the point is that there is less likelihood of mistakes if you get into the habit of creating surfaces in an ordered manner.

The practice of drawing 3DFACEs in a an ordered manner will also help to make all the surface normals point in the right direction when the drawing is exported to 3D Studio. While 3D Studio can compensate for missing faces by rendering both sides of each face, other rendering programs cannot perform this function, requiring the source geometry to be properly ordered.

VIEWING THE DRAWING

You can view a shaded version of the 3D drawing at any time with the SHADE command. The SHADE command displays a simple rendering of your 3D drawing.

While creating a 3D drawing you might find the numerous lines confusing. A shaded view of your drawing is helpful in checking for misplaced objects or gaps in entities. It can also help you visualize your drawing as you create it.

Before using the SHADE command it's helpful to change your viewport to an angled view. This type of view will show more of the 3D aspects of your drawing than an orthographic view. The VPOINT command can be used for this purpose.

VPOINT

The VPOINT command presents an angled view of your drawing.

> Command: **VPOINT**
> Rotate/<View point> <0.0000,0.0000,1.0000>: **1,1,1**

There are a few options as to how to specify your viewing location. The VPOINT command always looks at the point 0,0,0 (origin). You then specify an XYZ coordinate representing your viewpoint in space. The viewpoint points infinitely in the specified direction.

You can also specify your viewpoint by polar coordinates with the *Rotate* option. This is the most accurate way to define a location, or an alteration to an existing location. The XYZ coordinate is sometimes a little difficult to use as it is not easy to intuitively guess a viewing coordinate in terms of X, Y and Z, while the *Rotate* option is far more intuitive in the data it requires.

If you respond with ⟵⟞, a set of axes appears on the screen. The axes can be adjusted with your pointing device to interactively set a viewpoint. The interactive process is the quickest way to get an arbitrary 3D viewpoint of your drawing.

SHADE

The SHADE command displays a shaded version of your drawing on the screen. SHADE is convenient because it operates from within AutoCAD. The shaded picture you get from the SHADE command is not as realistic as a rendering from 3D Studio, it will give you an idea of how your drawing is shaping up.

Command: **SHADE**
Shading complete.

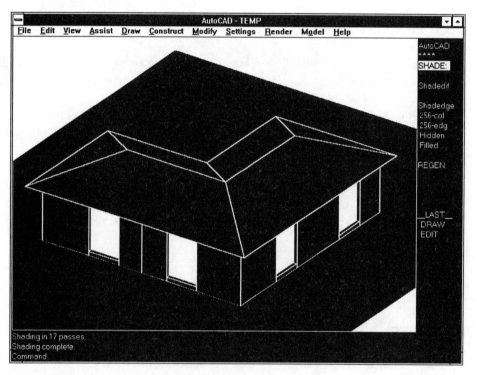

FIGURE 4-23. Drawing shaded with SHADE command.

The SHADE command first performs a REGEN of your drawing, then constructs the shaded image. To return to your wireframe drawing, perform a REGEN.

Command: **REGEN**

The wireframe will be redrawn, ready for further editing.

HIDE

The HIDE command can be used to hide the lines in the "back" of your drawing. When HIDE is used, the screen is redrawn without the lines in back. The HIDE command has no options.

Command: **HIDE**

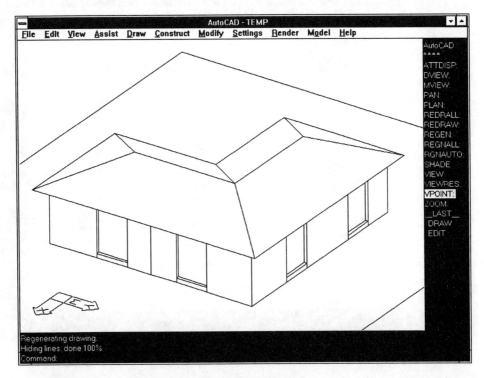

FIGURE 4-24. Lines hidden with HIDE command.

The HIDE process can be very slow on a large 3D drawing. In many cases the SHADE command will get a useful result on the screen much faster.

DVIEW

The DVIEW command is used to create a perspective view of a 3D drawing in AutoCAD. A perspective view can convey the design more clearly than an orthographic view, especially to non-technical persons.

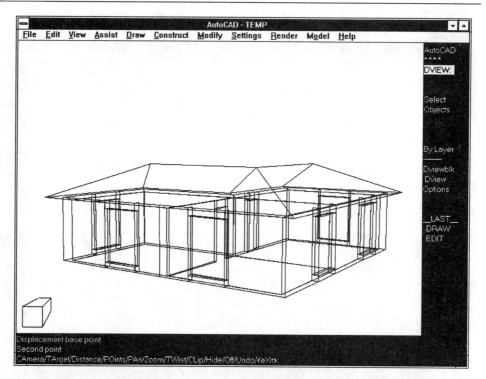

FIGURE 4-25. Perspective view of house model generated with DVIEW.

DVIEW provides more viewing controls than VPOINT, allowing you to view the model with a virtual camera. The camera settings determine the perspective view. The drawing can then be plotted or SHADEd as desired. You can tell if you are in DVIEW mode by checking for the perspective box at the lower left of the screen.

Command: **DVIEW**
Select objects: *(Pick an entity)*
CAmera/TArget/Distance/POints/PAn/Zoom/TWist/CLip/Hide/Off/Undo/
<eXit>:

Effective use of DVIEW requires some knowledge of the options available. If you learn the DVIEW options and plan your work with this command ahead of time, it will be much easier to get a working view of your drawing.

When you change a DVIEW option you will see a "ghost" image of your drawing which can be dragged around the screen. This is useful in setting viewpoints and other parameters. When you start DVIEW, you are asked to pick entities to be used in the ghost image. Choose the minimum number of entities needed to define the outer shape of the drawing. If you choose too many entities, the ghost image may move very slowly on the screen.

The CAmera and TArget options let you specify a location for the camera and its target. The target determines the direction of the camera.

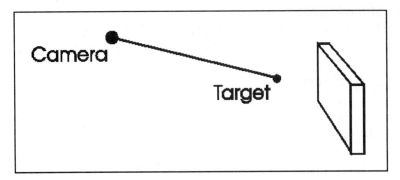

FIGURE 4-26. Camera and target.

The Distance option sets the distance from the camera to the target. To get a perspective view, the Distance option must be set to a value other than 1. A slider is displayed on the screen with the Distance option so the view can be interactively set.

The POints option allows you to enter both the camera and target positions with one command. This option is the most useful for setting up a working view.

```
Command: DVIEW
Select objects: (Pick entities for ghost image)
CAmera/TArget/Distance/POints/PAn/Zoom/TWist/CLip/Hide/Off/Undo/
<eXit>: PO
Enter target point <454.00, 340.65, 400.50>: .XY (Pick a point in XY plane)
of (need Z): 1600
Enter camera point <454.00, 340.65, 401.50>: .XY (Pick a point in XY plane)
of (need Z): 1750
```

You can pick a point in the X/Y plane, then enter an elevation for the Z value. This can make it easier for you to pick a camera and target that will work for your drawing. Note that a camera elevation of 1800mm or 6ft will approximate a standing person's eye level.

The PAn option moves both the camera and target in the specified direction, while the Zoom option changes the focal length of the camera to make the drawing appear closer. The TWist option tilts the camera.

The CLip option places a vertical plane through the drawing at a specified distance from the camera or target position. All lines in front of or behind the plane are discarded in the screen display. By varying the position of this plane it
is possible to take slices through your model at any point. The example given below places a plane 1000 units in front of the target point, resulting in everything in front of this plane being discarded.

```
Command: DVIEW
Select objects: (Pick an entity)
CAmera/TArget/Distance/POints/PAn/Zoom/TWist/CLip/Hide/Off/Undo/
<eXit>: CL
```

Back/Front/<Off>: **F**
Eye/<Distance from target> <2105.19>: **1000**
CAmera/TArget/Distance/POints/PAn/Zoom/TWist/CLip/Hide/Off/Undo/
<eXit>: **X**
Regenerating drawing.

The CLip option is not used in the course of most AutoCAD work, but can be useful occasionally for a special purpose.

The Hide option hides any lines that would be hidden if the 3D drawing were solid. The eXit option exits the DVIEW command but leaves the perspective view on the screen. The Off option turns off the perspective view and returns you to an orthographic view.

The DVIEW options are very easy to use when making minor adjustments to an existing viewing position. The most difficult part is the initial task of getting close to the viewpoint you want.

For the best results, use the POints command first to approximate the desired view of your drawing. You can then use other options to fine-tune the view. Use the Distance option to move the camera closer or further away from the target, and use PAn to move the view slightly within the viewport. If your computer takes too long to drag and redraw images on the screen, try turning off some of your drawing layers.

When finished setting up the view, you can plot or SHADE the picture.

While DVIEW is active, the AutoCAD commands PAN and ZOOM will not work. If you must perform these functions while in a DVIEW view, use the PAn and Zoom options from within DVIEW. You can tell if DVIEW is active by checking if the perspective box still appears at the lower left of the screen.

EXPORTING THE DRAWING

Once a drawing has been created in 3D, it must be exported to DXF format, then imported to 3D Studio.

DXF Export

The DXFOUT command is used to export 3D drawings. A DXF file can then be imported to 3D Studio.

The DXFOUT command is used to export a 3D drawing to DXF format.

Command: **DXFOUT**

The Create DXF File dialog box appears, as shown in Figure 4-27. This dialog box is for choosing an output filename and subdirectory for the DXF file. Choose a directory and enter a filename. DXF files for later use in 3D Studio should be saved in your 3D Studio MESHES directory.

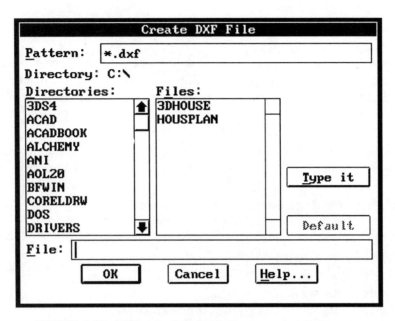

FIGURE 4-27. DXF output dialog box.

When you exit the dialog box, you will see the following prompt:

Enter decimal places of accuracy (0 to 16)/Entities/Binary <6>: **E**

This prompt reflects the two methods that can be used to export the drawing, the *Entities* method and the *Accuracy* method. The Entities method asks you to select, with a window or fence, only those entities on the screen which you want to export. If you do not want to export the entire drawing, use this method. But be aware that blocks will not export with the Entities method; they must be exploded first in order to export them.

To use the Entities method, set layers so that anything you want to export is displayed on screen, and explode blocks that contain entities you want to export. This should have been done before you entered the DXFOUT command.

Enter decimal places of accuracy (0 to 16)/Entities/Binary <6>: **E**
Select Objects: *(use a selection tool to select what you want to export)*
Select Objects: ⟨⎯⟩
Enter decimal places of accuracy (0 to 16)/Entities/Binary <6>: ⟨⎯⟩

The Accuracy method is simpler. It exports every entity on the screen, including unexploded
blocks, as well as all entities on layers that are turned off or frozen.

Enter decimal places of accuracy (0 to 16)/Entities/Binary <6>:

Wait a few moments as the DXF file is created.

CREATING A 3D DRAWING

The first step in creating a 3D drawing is to work out the layering system. Remember that when the drawing is exported to 3D Studio, each layer will become a separate object. For this reason you will need a layering system quite different from your usual 2D approach.

Before using the computer, jot down your proposed layering system on a sheet of paper. Figure 4-28 shows a sample layers list for a simple drawing of a house.

```
CEILING - internal ceilings
ROOF   - external roof
OWALL  - outer walls
IWALL  - inner walls
GLASS  - glass window panels
FLOOR  - internal floor
EAVES  - external eaves (under roof edges)
DOOR   - front door
GROUND  - ground plane
TEMP   - used for reference lines
```

FIGURE 4-28. Sample layers listing.

Note any such items which appear several times in the drawing, such as windows and doors. It's easier to copy a portion of the drawing, and perhaps change it, than it is to create it from scratch. Copying and altering will save you drawing time.

Layers

Before drawing the 3D objects, create the appropriate layers for your work. If you've prepared ahead of time this should be a simple step. Layers are created with the LAYER command.

You can use the LAYER command and either the NEW or MAKE options. Note that colors must be defined separately when using NEW, though multiple layers can be created at one time. With MAKE, only one layer at a time can be created, though it is set automatically to be the current drawing layer.

Once you have created a few 3D AutoCAD drawings, you will find that you can use the same layering system over and over again. As you become more proficient with AutoCAD you can automate your layer creation with a script file.

Building a 3D Architectural Drawing

In working out which commands you'll need to build your drawing, remember that you can use more than one command to build a single part. For example, you may find that you need to use two or more commands to build a roof. This works as long as all the roof entities are on the same layer.

In this section we will discuss the general approach to creating a 3D architectural drawing. Later in this chapter a detailed tutorial will show you how to use the commands to build a simple 3D drawing of a house.

Outer Walls. The best place to start your 3D house drawing is with the outer walls. These can usually be created quite quickly and can then act as good reference geometry for all subsequent drawing. One way to draw outer walls is to draw the outline with a PLINE then extrude the object with CHANGE, CHPROP or ELEV. For walls with windows or doors, use solid modeling to poke the window and door holes from primitives.

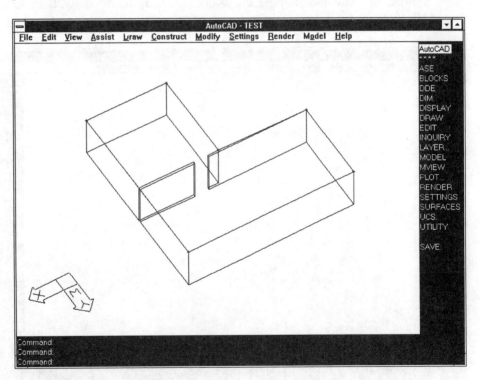

FIGURE 4-29. Inner and outer walls.

Inner Walls. The inner walls can be constructed in the same manner as the outer walls, except they should be created on a different layer. Be sure to check whether the inner walls should have the same height as the outer walls. This is not always the case. If the heights are different, remember this later when it comes time to deal with the roof and ceiling.

Floor and Ceiling. The OSNAP commands are very handy for creating the floor and ceiling. An extruded LINE or PLINE makes an excellent floor or ceiling. Once these items have been created, it's a good time to check the validity of your drawing by doing a quick SHADE of the drawing.

Roof and Eaves. Pitched roof panels are often a challenge for AutoCAD users. One convenient approach is to create temporary reference geometry to represent the edges of the roof. You then create a 3DFACE for each roof panel, using reference geometry to snap to the correct points.

Put the reference lines in the TEMP layer so they can easily be hidden when they're no longer needed. Draw one set of reference lines for the eaves, and another for the roof.

If the location of the eaves line is not given, it may be assumed to be 15 to 20 inches out from the location of the outer wall. If we draw a polyline around this eaves line on the ground, and another for the position of the apex of the roof, we will have enough data defined to draw the roof panels. Note that we should draw both reference lines as polylines so we can move them vertically as single entities.

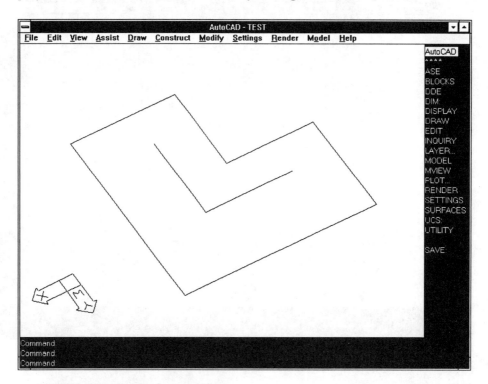

FIGURE 4-30. Roof reference lines.

The eaves line will usually be at the same height as the outer wall. The apex line is located at some height above this, depending on the pitch angle of the roof. One simple way to determine this height is to draw a small pencil-and-paper sketch of the geometry to determine, at the given pitch angle, how much higher the apex point is above the eaves point. Once determined, use the AutoCAD MOVE command and relative coordinates to move the lines into position, if necessary.

When the reference lines have been placed, it's then a simple matter to set OSNAP to END and use the 3DFACE command to draw each roof panel.

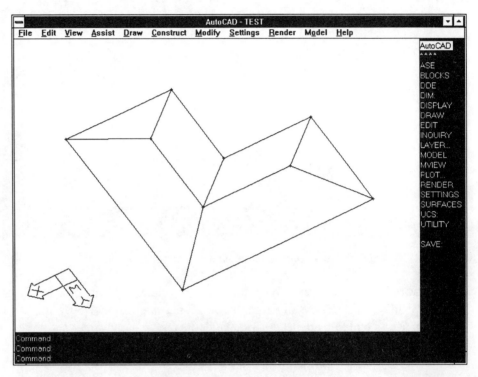

FIGURE 4-31. Roof panels drawn with reference lines as snap points for 3DFACE command.

The eaves can then be drawn with the 3DFACE command. In this case, the outer wall and eaves reference line can be used as snap points.

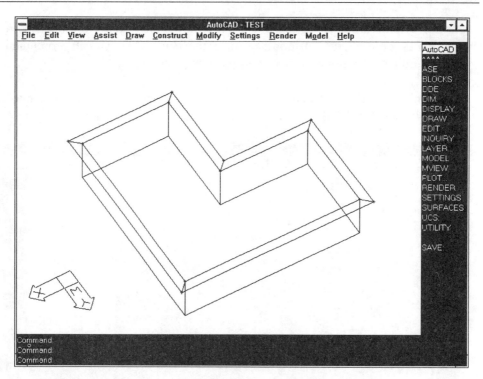

FIGURE 4-32. Eaves drawn with 3DFACE command.

Doors and Windows. Doors and windows can be drawn very simply or in great detail depending on the type of presentation. For a mass model only the volume and rough shape of a building are necessary, and doors and windows may not be required at all.

Even if you plan to include doors and windows, it is usually not necessary to include all the real-life detail in a 3D drawing. Much of the detail will not be detectable in the final rendering, especially when the view is far away. However, if you plan to walk in the front door of a house, a considerable level of detail will be needed, including doorknobs and panels.

For very simple doors and windows, you need not make window and door holes in the walls. You can leave the walls solid and draw a 3DFACE of the appropriate size for each door and window. You then place each face just in front of the outer wall panels. They need only be a couple of units in front of the wall - just enough so the renderer can differentiate between the two panels. This approach works well for presentations where the camera will not be going too close to the model.

Drawing fully detailed windows and doors can be a tedious and time consuming process. One useful technique is to create a single highly detailed item, then use it over and over again with minor variations. In AutoCAD the STRETCH command can be used to stretch an item to new sizes. In 3D Studio, the object modification commands can be used for the same purpose. Once you have a detailed door or window, keep it for use in future drawings.

There are also several third-party packages that include 3D window frames, doorframes and furniture for AutoCAD. Your AutoCAD dealer or Autodesk can tell you more about these packages.

Detail. Small detail elements improve the level of realism in a drawing. For example, guttering and downpipes provide an extra level of interest. While you may not consciously notice such things on a real house, you do notice something's amiss when they're not present.

Extra elements can also provide additional color within an image. Some brightly painted guttering can help lift an otherwise drab brick wall, both in the real world and on your computer drawing.

Paths and driveways can be easily added as 3DFACE elements placed horizontally, rendered with a concrete or bitumen material. Fences can be included to show the edges of the building site. A fence can quickly be created as lines with thickness equal to the fence height.

Additional detail can be most easily provided in the form of some of the growing number of third-party libraries of 3D elements on the market. This is the easiest way to obtain plumbing fixtures and interior furnishings, as well as basic cars and people to populate your building.

Ground. When dealing with buildings it is usually a good idea to incorporate a large flat horizontal face to represent the ground. This has a number of positive effects. It provides a surface on which shadows can fall, and also provides a reference plane for viewing. People expect buildings to sit on the ground, so providing an obvious ground plane can make the drawing seem more realistic than just a house sitting in the middle of empty space.

A ground plane also helps to cut down on the flat background area. If, say, you provide a light blue background to represent the sky, the lower region of this background will be blanked out by a ground plane, resulting in an image which appears more logical. A ground plane can be added in either AutoCAD or 3D Studio.

Limitations in 3D Drawing

Provided valid 3D geometry is used in AutoCAD, there should be no problems exporting the drawing to 3D Studio.

Much of this information will be helpful to you only when you move on to more advanced 3D drawings. However, it's a good idea to familiarize yourself with these limitations so you'll recognize a particular problem when you encounter it.

Lines

When a drawing is imported into 3D Studio by way of a DXF file, 3D Studio will only recognize true 3D entities. For example, a LINE or PLINE in AutoCAD which has no thickness will be ignored by 3D Studio as it is not considered valid 3D geometry. Conversely, a LINE or PLINE with thickness is regarded as valid 3D geometry. If you import a drawing into 3D Studio and some of the geometry disappears, most likely it was drawn incorrectly in AutoCAD.

Blocks

Versions of 3D Studio prior to Release 3 were unable to accept AutoCAD BLOCK entities, so if you are using an early 3D Studio version you may encounter this limitation. If you do, the solution is to EXPLODE all the BLOCK entities in AutoCAD prior to exporting a DXF file for transfer to 3D Studio.

Closed Polylines

One area where interesting results can arise with 3D geometry is when dealing with closed polylines. A closed polyline is translated as a surface when exported to 3D Studio. Depending on your point of view, this could be either good or bad. If you are aware of this, it becomes a very powerful feature and a good way to define quite complex geometry in AutoCAD with minimal effort. If unaware of this, peculiar problems can occur, as shown in the following example.

The drawing below shows a situation where a closed polyline is interfering with valid 3D geometry. This file shows a window panel drawn over a wall, where a closed polyline has been drawn as a reference for positioning the window in AutoCAD.

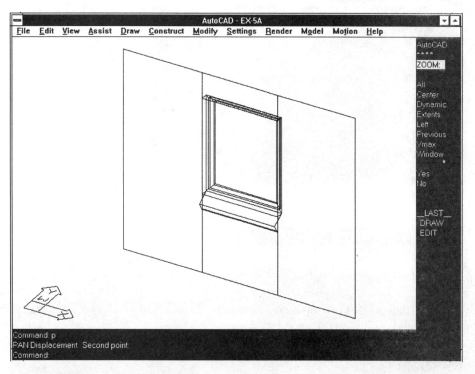

FIGURE 4-33. Window panel drawn over a wall.

When this drawing is rendered with the AutoCAD SHADE command, there appear to be no problems.

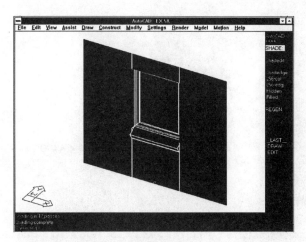

FIGURE 4-34. Drawing rendered with SHADE command

However, when we export this file to DXF, import it to 3D Studio and render it, a problem becomes evident. The window frame has vanished.

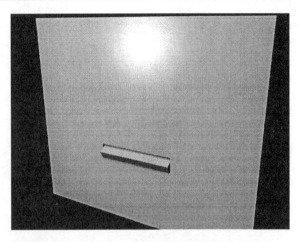

FIGURE 4-35. Drawing rendered in 3D Studio.

The closed polyline has been interpreted as a face, causing all the geometry behind it to be hidden. The solution is to go back into AutoCAD and use the EXPLODE command on the polyline to convert it into four separate lines. The file, when exported to 3D Studio, will render correctly.

FIGURE 4-36. Drawing with EXPLODEd lines, rendered in 3D Studio.

Faces Coincident

Another problem often encountered when drawing in AutoCAD that two faces may occupy exactly the same place. Two faces in the same location are said to be *coincident*. Although this is impossible in real life it can easily happen in a 3D drawing. This becomes a problem if different materials are applied to the two faces in 3D Studio.

When the two faces occupy the same location the 3D Studio renderer has difficulty deciding which one should be in front, and may randomly choose one face or another. If coincident faces have different materials assigned to them, two renderings of the same model may show a different color where the faces lie. In an animated sequence this color difference may cause the face to "flash" between frames.

In practice it is difficult to spot coincident faces in AutoCAD. This problem is usually discovered when preliminary renderings are made in 3D Studio. You can delete individual faces in 3D Studio, but it's often difficult to locate the face that's causing the problem.

Gaps in Edges

Inaccurate drawing will usually result in gaps between 3DFACE entities where they are supposed to meet. A gap can appear quite small and innocent when drawing in AutoCAD, but becomes very obvious once the drawing is rendered in 3D Studio.

The only way to avoid gaps is to make liberal use of the Object Snap (OSNAP) facilities in AutoCAD. OSNAP will help you ensure that geometry is accurately drawn and vertices are exactly coincident. Because OSNAP snaps to the nearest specified point, if you inadvertently select the wrong point the mistake will be obvious right away.

In trying to avoid gaps in your drawings you can also view your model from another viewpoint with the VPOINT command. This will help you see if all your lines are going where they should. You can also use the SHADE command to check for missing faces or gaps.

Tips

If you're planning to build 3D drawings often, then it may be a good idea to automate parts of the process where possible. For example, an automated layer routine will speed up your preparation for drawing.

You may also find it useful to keep parts of your drawings for use in the future. Any geometry that takes a long time to draw is worth keeping to save work in the future.

EXERCISES

Exercise 1

Use each of the commands below with the ELEV command to produce a 3D entity. Before beginning, make a layer for each entity. Place each entity on the appropriate layer.

_____	ARC	3D arc
_____	CIRCLE	Cylinder
_____	SOLID	Rectangular prism
_____	TEXT	3D text
_____	TRACE	Rectangular prism
_____	PLINE	One or more planar surfaces
_____	LINE	Planar surface

When finished making the entities, export the drawing to DXF format. Call the export file EXTRUDED.DXF.

Exercise 2

Look at the 3D entities below. Work out which AutoCAD commands you would use to create each one. In some cases there may be more than one way to make the object.

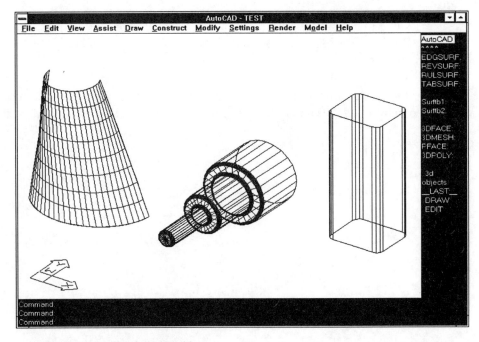

FIGURE 4-37. Surfaced entities.

Exercise 3

Use one of the surfacing commands to make one of the surfaced entities above. The surfacing commands are REVSURF, RULESURF, TABSURF and EDGESURF. Refer to the appropriate sections of this chapter for information on how to use these commands.

When finished making the entity, export the drawing to DXF format. Call the export file SURFACED.DXF.

TUTORIAL

In this tutorial you'll use the AutoCAD 3D commands described in this chapter to create a simple house drawing.

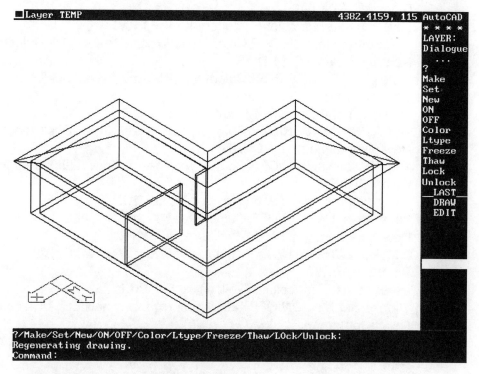

FIGURE 4-38. Simple house drawing.

1. Layers

Open a new AutoCAD drawing. Use the LAYER command to make the layers as follows:

Command: **LAYER**

?/Make/Set/New/ON/OFF/Color/Ltype/Freeze/Thaw/LOck/Unlock: **N**
New layer name(s): **2DPLAN**
?/Make/Set/New/ON/OFF/Color/Ltype/Freeze/Thaw/LOck/Unlock: **C**
Color: **WHITE**
Layer name(s) for color 7 (white) <0>: **2DPLAN**
?/Make/Set/New/ON/OFF/Color/Ltype/Freeze/Thaw/LOck/Unlock: **N**
New layer name(s): **CEILING**
?/Make/Set/New/ON/OFF/Color/Ltype/Freeze/Thaw/LOck/Unlock: **C**
Color: **CYAN**
Layer name(s) for color 4 (cyan) <0>: **CEILING**
?/Make/Set/New/ON/OFF/Color/Ltype/Freeze/Thaw/LOck/Unlock: **N**
New layer name(s): **DOOR**
?/Make/Set/New/ON/OFF/Color/Ltype/Freeze/Thaw/LOck/Unlock: **C**
Color: **BLUE**
Layer name(s) for color 5 (blue) <0>: **DOOR**
?/Make/Set/New/ON/OFF/Color/Ltype/Freeze/Thaw/LOck/Unlock: **N**
New layer name(s): **EAVES**
?/Make/Set/New/ON/OFF/Color/Ltype/Freeze/Thaw/LOck/Unlock: **C**
Color: **MAGENTA**
Layer name(s) for color 6 (magenta) <0>: **EAVES**
?/Make/Set/New/ON/OFF/Color/Ltype/Freeze/Thaw/LOck/Unlock: **N**
New layer name(s): **FLOOR**
?/Make/Set/New/ON/OFF/Color/Ltype/Freeze/Thaw/LOck/Unlock: **C**
Color: **CYAN**
Layer name(s) for color 4 (cyan) <0>: **FLOOR**
?/Make/Set/New/ON/OFF/Color/Ltype/Freeze/Thaw/LOck/Unlock: **N**
New layer name(s): **GROUND**
?/Make/Set/New/ON/OFF/Color/Ltype/Freeze/Thaw/LOck/Unlock: **C**
Color: **GREEN**
Layer name(s) for color 3 (green) <0>: **GROUND**
?/Make/Set/New/ON/OFF/Color/Ltype/Freeze/Thaw/LOck/Unlock: **N**
New layer name(s): IWALL
?/Make/Set/New/ON/OFF/Color/Ltype/Freeze/Thaw/LOck/Unlock: **C**
Color: **YELLOW**
Layer name(s) for color 2 (yellow) <0>: **IWALL**
?/Make/Set/New/ON/OFF/Color/Ltype/Freeze/Thaw/LOck/Unlock: **N**
New layer name(s): **OWALL**
?/Make/Set/New/ON/OFF/Color/Ltype/Freeze/Thaw/LOck/Unlock: **C**
Color: **RED**
Layer name(s) for color 1 (red) <0>: **OWALL**
?/Make/Set/New/ON/OFF/Color/Ltype/Freeze/Thaw/LOck/Unlock: **N**
New layer name(s): **ROOF**
?/Make/Set/New/ON/OFF/Color/Ltype/Freeze/Thaw/LOck/Unlock: **C**
Color: **BLUE**
Layer name(s) for color 5 (blue) <0>: **ROOF**
?/Make/Set/New/ON/OFF/Color/Ltype/Freeze/Thaw/LOck/Unlock: ⏎

2. Outer Walls

Next you'll draw in the outer walls using a wall height (line thickness) of 2500 units.

```
Command: ELEV
New current elevation <0.0000>: 0
New current thickness <0.0000>: 2500

Command: LAYER
?/Make/Set/New/ON/OFF/Color/Ltype/Freeze/Thaw/LOck/Unlock: S
New current layer <0>: OWALL
?/Make/Set/New/ON/OFF/Color/Ltype/Freeze/Thaw/LOck/Unlock: ⏎

Command: PLINE
From point: 0,0
Current line-width is 0.0000
Arc/Close/Halfwidth/Length/Undo/Width/<Endpoint of line>: 5000,0
Arc/Close/Halfwidth/Length/Undo/Width/<Endpoint of line>: 5000,-5000
Arc/Close/Halfwidth/Length/Undo/Width/<Endpoint of line>: 10000,-5000
Arc/Close/Halfwidth/Length/Undo/Width/<Endpoint of line>: 10000,5000
Arc/Close/Halfwidth/Length/Undo/Width/<Endpoint of line>: 0,5000
Arc/Close/Halfwidth/Length/Undo/Width/<Endpoint of line>: C
```

Perform a zoom to make the drawing easier to see.

```
Command: ZOOM
All/Center/Dynamic/Extents/Left/Previous/Vmax/Window/<Scale(X/XP)>: E
Regenerating drawing.

Command: ZOOM
All/Center/Dynamic/Extents/Left/Previous/Vmax/Window/<Scale(X/XP)>: 0.9X
```

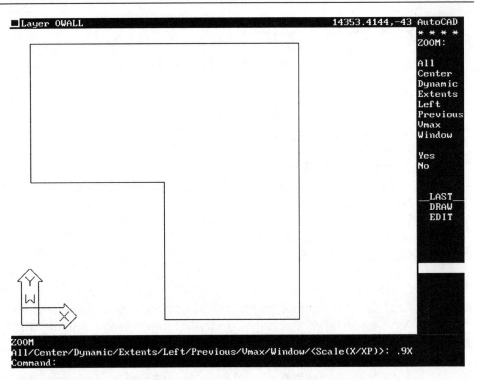

FIGURE 4-39. Outer walls.

Use the AutoCAD VPOINT command to view the external walls from an angle. Also use the SHADE command to better see the solidity of the drawing.

Command: **VPOINT**
Rotate/<View point> <0.0000,0.0000,1.0000>: **-1,-1.25,1**
Regenerating drawing.

Command: **SHADE**
Shading complete.

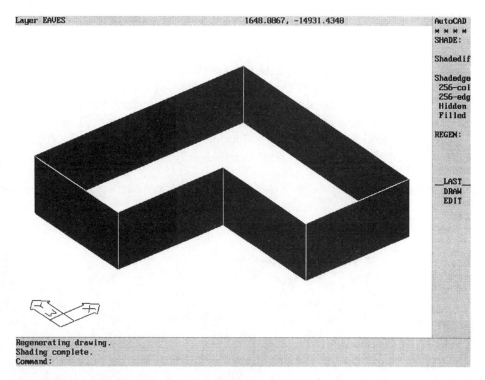

FIGURE 4-40. Shaded view of outer walls.

Perform a REGEN to return to the wireframe drawing.

Command: **REGEN**

4. Inner Walls

Next you'll add internal walls with a height of 2400 units. Note that the height of the inner walls is 100 units lower than the height of the outer walls.

Command: **ELEV**
New current elevation <0.0000>: **0**
New current thickness <2500.0000>: **2400**

Command: **LAYER**
?/Make/Set/New/ON/OFF/Color/Ltype/Freeze/Thaw/LOck/Unlock: **S**
New current layer <OWALL>: **IWALL**
?/Make/Set/New/ON/OFF/Color/Ltype/Freeze/Thaw/LOck/Unlock: ⬅

Command: **PLINE**
From point: **250,250**
Current line-width is 0.0000
Arc/Close/Halfwidth/Length/Undo/Width/<Endpoint of line>: **5856,250**
Arc/Close/Halfwidth/Length/Undo/Width/<Endpoint of line>: **5856,140**
Arc/Close/Halfwidth/Length/Undo/Width/<Endpoint of line>: **5250,140**

Arc/Close/Halfwidth/Length/Undo/Width/<Endpoint of line>: **5250,-4750**
Arc/Close/Halfwidth/Length/Undo/Width/<Endpoint of line>: **9750,-4750**
Arc/Close/Halfwidth/Length/Undo/Width/<Endpoint of line>: **9750,140**
Arc/Close/Halfwidth/Length/Undo/Width/<Endpoint of line>: **6676,140**
Arc/Close/Halfwidth/Length/Undo/Width/<Endpoint of line>: **6676,250**
Arc/Close/Halfwidth/Length/Undo/Width/<Endpoint of line>: **9750,250**
Arc/Close/Halfwidth/Length/Undo/Width/<Endpoint of line>: **9750,4750**
Arc/Close/Halfwidth/Length/Undo/Width/<Endpoint of line>: **250,4750**
Arc/Close/Halfwidth/Length/Undo/Width/<Endpoint of line>: **C**

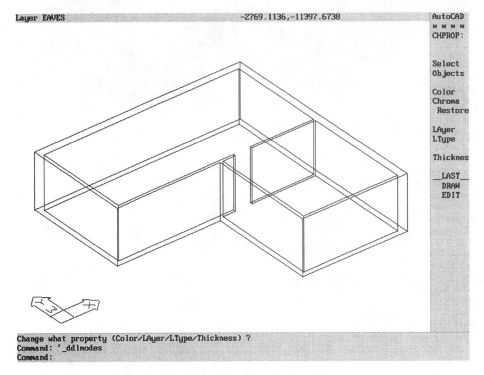

FIGURE 4-41. Inner walls and outer walls.

Note that the color difference makes the drawing easier to understand.

5. Floor and Ceiling

The floor and ceiling panels connect to the edges of the inner walls. First you'll make the ceiling as a single PLINE with an elevation of 2400 and no thickness.

To make it easier to create the ceiling, you'll turn off all the drawing layers except the CEILING layer.

Command: **LAYER**
?/Make/Set/New/ON/OFF/Color/Ltype/Freeze/Thaw/LOck/Unlock: **S**
New current layer <IWALL>: **CEILING**
?/Make/Set/New/ON/OFF/Color/Ltype/Freeze/Thaw/LOck/Unlock: **F**

Layer name(s) to Freeze: *
Cannot freeze layer CEILING. It is the CURRENT layer.
?/Make/Set/New/ON/OFF/Color/Ltype/Freeze/Thaw/LOck/Unlock: ⬅

Next, set the elevation and thickness for the ceiling entity.

Command: **ELEV**
New current elevation <0.0000>: **2400**
New current thickness <2400.0000>: **0**

Command: **PLINE**
From point: **250,250**
Current line-width is 0.0000
Arc/Close/Halfwidth/Length/Undo/Width/<Endpoint of line>: **5250,250**
Arc/Close/Halfwidth/Length/Undo/Width/<Endpoint of line>: **5250,-4750**
Arc/Close/Halfwidth/Length/Undo/Width/<Endpoint of line>: **9750,-4750**
Arc/Close/Halfwidth/Length/Undo/Width/<Endpoint of line>: **9750,4750**
Arc/Close/Halfwidth/Length/Undo/Width/<Endpoint of line>: **250,4750**
Arc/Close/Halfwidth/Length/Undo/Width/<Endpoint of line>: **C**

Now use the same process to create the floor panels.

Command: **LAYER**
?/Make/Set/New/ON/OFF/Color/Ltype/Freeze/Thaw/LOck/Unlock: **F**
Layer name(s) to Freeze: **CEILING**
Cannot freeze layer CEILING. It is the CURRENT layer.
?/Make/Set/New/ON/OFF/Color/Ltype/Freeze/Thaw/LOck/Unlock: **T**
Layer name(s) to Thaw: **FLOOR**
?/Make/Set/New/ON/OFF/Color/Ltype/Freeze/Thaw/LOck/Unlock: **S**
New current layer <CEILING>: **FLOOR**
?/Make/Set/New/ON/OFF/Color/Ltype/Freeze/Thaw/LOck/Unlock: ⬅

Command: **ELEV**
New current elevation <2400.0000>: **0**
New current thickness <0.0000>: **0**

Command: **PLINE**
From point: **250,250**
Current line-width is 0.0000
Arc/Close/Halfwidth/Length/Undo/Width/<Endpoint of line>: **5250,250**
Arc/Close/Halfwidth/Length/Undo/Width/<Endpoint of line>: **5250,-4750**
Arc/Close/Halfwidth/Length/Undo/Width/<Endpoint of line>: **9750,-4750**
Arc/Close/Halfwidth/Length/Undo/Width/<Endpoint of line>: **9750,4750**
Arc/Close/Halfwidth/Length/Undo/Width/<Endpoint of line>: **250,4750**
Arc/Close/Halfwidth/Length/Undo/Width/<Endpoint of line>: **C**

6. Roof and Eaves Reference Lines

A pitched roof is one case where the 3DFACE command comes in handy. When using the 3DFACE command it is essential that you have reference points already drawn. For the roof and eaves you will draw reference lines on a new layer called TEMP.

First you'll create the new layer TEMP.

```
Command: LAYER
?/Make/Set/New/ON/OFF/Color/Ltype/Freeze/Thaw/LOck/Unlock: M
New current layer <FLOOR>: TEMP
?/Make/Set/New/ON/OFF/Color/Ltype/Freeze/Thaw/LOck/Unlock: C
Color: MAGENTA
Layer name(s) for color 6 (magenta) <TEMP>: TEMP
?/Make/Set/New/ON/OFF/Color/Ltype/Freeze/Thaw/LOck/Unlock: ⏎
```

Next you'll turn off all the other drawing layers.

```
Command: LAYER
?/Make/Set/New/ON/OFF/Color/Ltype/Freeze/Thaw/LOck/Unlock: F
Layer name(s) to Freeze: *
Cannot freeze layer TEMP.  It is the CURRENT layer.
?/Make/Set/New/ON/OFF/Color/Ltype/Freeze/Thaw/LOck/Unlock: ⏎
```

Now you'll draw reference lines for the eaves.

```
Command: ELEV
New current elevation <0.0000>: 2500
New current thickness <0.0000>: 0

Command: PLINE
From point: -500,-500
Current line-width is 0.0000
Arc/Close/Halfwidth/Length/Undo/Width/<Endpoint of line>: 4500,-500
Arc/Close/Halfwidth/Length/Undo/Width/<Endpoint of line>: 4500,-5500
Arc/Close/Halfwidth/Length/Undo/Width/<Endpoint of line>: 10500,-5500
Arc/Close/Halfwidth/Length/Undo/Width/<Endpoint of line>: 10500,5500
Arc/Close/Halfwidth/Length/Undo/Width/<Endpoint of line>: -500,5500
Arc/Close/Halfwidth/Length/Undo/Width/<Endpoint of line>: C
```

Two more lines will further define the pitched roof.

```
Command: ELEV
New current elevation <2500.0000>: 3775
New current thickness <0.0000>: 0

Command: PLINE
```

From point: **2500,2500**
Current line-width is 0.0000
Arc/Close/Halfwidth/Length/Undo/Width/<Endpoint of line>: **7500,2500**
Arc/Close/Halfwidth/Length/Undo/Width/<Endpoint of line>: **7500,-2500**
Arc/Close/Halfwidth/Length/Undo/Width/<Endpoint of line>: ⟵

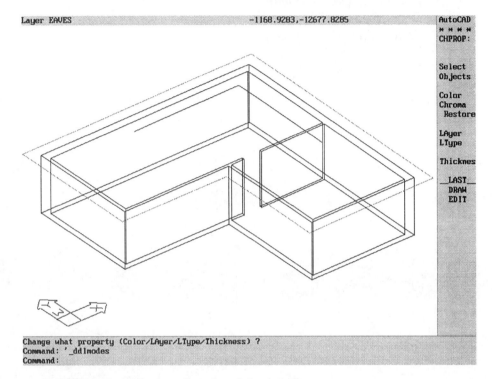

FIGURE 4-42. Reference lines for pitched roof.

7. Roof and Eaves

With the reference lines, you can use 3DFACE to draw the eaves and pitched roof panels. With the 3DFACE command you can use the endpoints of the reference lines to snap the corners of each face. First you must turn snap on.

Command: **OSNAP**
Object snap modes: **END**

Next you'll change the layer to the eaves layer.

Command: **LAYER**
?/Make/Set/New/ON/OFF/Color/Ltype/Freeze/Thaw/LOck/Unlock: **T**
Layer name(s) to Thaw: **EAVES**
?/Make/Set/New/ON/OFF/Color/Ltype/Freeze/Thaw/LOck/Unlock: **S**
New current layer <TEMP>: **EAVES**
?/Make/Set/New/ON/OFF/Color/Ltype/Freeze/Thaw/LOck/Unlock: **T**
Layer name(s) to Thaw: **OWALLS**
?/Make/Set/New/ON/OFF/Color/Ltype/Freeze/Thaw/LOck/Unlock: ⟵

Now use the 3DFACE command to draw the eaves faces. Click on four corners of each face, then press ⬅— to finish drawing the face. See Figure 4-43.

Command: **3DFACE**
First point: *(Pick a point)*
Second point: *(Pick a point)*
Third point: *(Pick a point)*
Fourth point: *(Pick a point)*
Third point: ⬅—

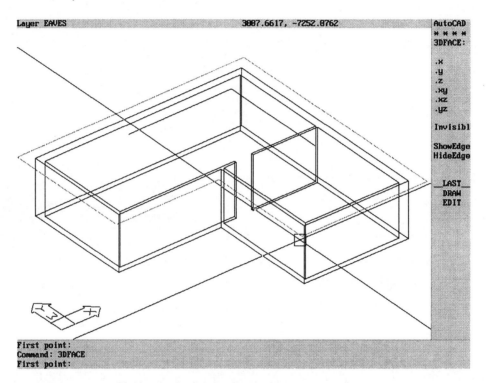

FIGURE 4-43. Picking endpoints to draw eaves.

The eaves are now complete. Perform a quick check of the geometry using the SHADE command.

Command: **SHADE**
Shading complete.

Now repeat the same procedure to draw the roof panels. Use the 3DFACE command to draw the pitched roof faces. Some roof faces have three corners instead of four. When asked the fourth point on these panels, click on the first point chosen.

When you've drawn the roof panels, the 3D drawing is complete. Thaw all layers to look at the drawing.

Command: **LAYER**

?/Make/Set/New/ON/OFF/Color/Ltype/Freeze/Thaw/LOck/Unlock: **T**
Layer name(s) to Thaw: *
?/Make/Set/New/ON/OFF/Color/Ltype/Freeze/Thaw/LOck/Unlock: ⬅

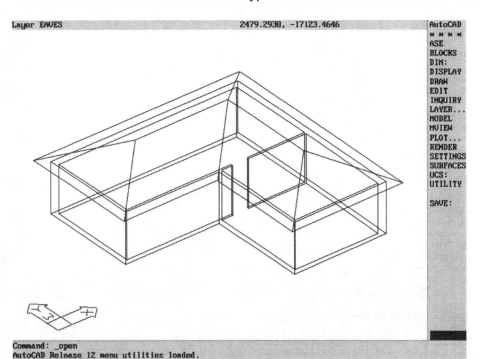

FIGURE 4-44. Roof panels and completed drawing.

9. Checking for errors

Look carefully at your drawing to see if there are any mistakes or problems with the drawing. To further check for drawing errors, return to the plan view of your drawing.

Command: **VPOINT**
Rotate/<View point> <-1.0000,-1.0000,1.0000>: **0,0,1**

Look for any out-of-place lines, as shown in Figure 4-45.

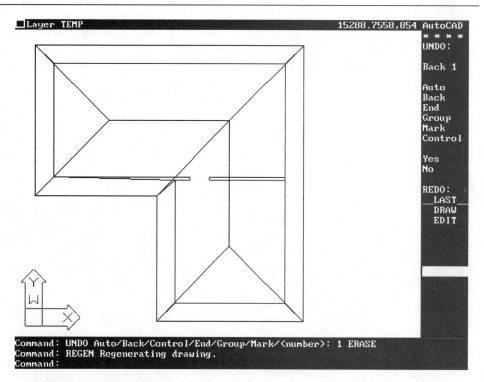

FIGURE 4-45. House model in plan view.

If you find any mistakes, erase the incorrect lines and repeat the appropriate step in this tutorial.

8. SHADE Check

Once you've checked the wireframe drawing, you can perform a further check with the SHADE command.

Command: **SHADE**
Shading complete.

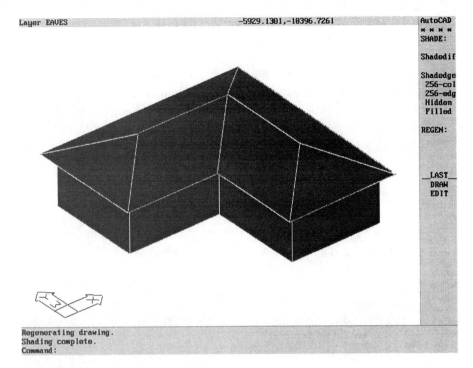

FIGURE 4-46. Shaded house model.

9. Delete Reference Lines

If you like, you can delete the eave and apex reference lines before saving or exporting the drawing. Because these lines are the only entities on the TEMP layer, you can freeze all layers except TEMP to make it easy to pick the reference lines for erasure. Then you can thaw all the layers.

> Command: **LAYER**
> ?/Make/Set/New/ON/OFF/Color/Ltype/Freeze/Thaw/LOck/Unlock: **S**
> New current layer <ROOF>: **TEMP**
> ?/Make/Set/New/ON/OFF/Color/Ltype/Freeze/Thaw/LOck/Unlock: **F**
> Layer name(s) to Freeze: *
> ?/Make/Set/New/ON/OFF/Color/Ltype/Freeze/Thaw/LOck/Unlock: ⏎
>
> Command: **ERASE**
> Select objects: *(Pick apex line)*
> Select objects: *(Pick eave line)*
> Select objects: ⏎

Next you'll thaw the layers.

> Command: **LAYER**
> ?/Make/Set/New/ON/OFF/Color?Ltype/Freeze/Thaw/LOck/Unlock: **T**
> Layer name(s) to Thaw: *
> ?/Make/Set/New/ON/OFF/Color/Ltype/Freeze/Thaw/LOck/Unlock: ⏎

10. Prepare to Export to DXF

Before making the DXF, there is one more detail that needs correcting. The inner and outer walls of the house are made of continuous PLINEs. One peculiarity of 3D Studio's DXF import function is that closed plines are "filled in" upon import. 3D Studio creates faces to turn closed PLINEs into planar surfaces, and if the PLINEs were extruded into 3D entities in AutoCAD the top and bottom of the entities will be capped. This is often a very useful feature, allowing the modeling of complex planar surfaces just by defining the boundaries of the surface with a closed PLINE in AutoCAD, and then DXFing the closed PLINE to 3D Studio.

For the house, however, we already have a ceiling and floor, and we don't want 3D Studio to cap the inner and outer walls with excess faces, so we will explode the plines that make the walls.

Command: **EXPLODE**
Select Objects: (use a crossing window that crosses only the inner and outer
        walls)
Select Objects: ⬅

11. Export to DXF

The last step is to save the drawing and export it to DXF format.

Command: **SAVE**
Save current changes as: **3DHOUSE**
Current drawing name set to **3DHOUSE**

Command: **DXFOUT**
(Choose the 3D Studio MESHES directory. Enter output filename
3DHOUSE.)
Enter decimal places of accuracy (0 to 16)/Entities/Binary <6>: **B**

The 3D drawing has now bee saved to the MESHES directory, and can be imported into 3D Studio.

CHAPTER

5

3D STUDIO
BASICS

In the last chapter you learned how to make a 3D AutoCAD model. These models can now be brought into 3D Studio.

In 3D Studio the model can be *rendered*. Rendering is the process of coloring and shading a model to make it look more real and to give the viewer a sense of what the design will look like when built.

The AutoCAD SHADE command provides a simple rendering. This command is useful for checking the validity of a 3D model, but is limited to very simple colors and shading.

With 3D Studio you can apply use more complex textures, such as brick, carpeting and wallpaper. You can have more flexibility in lighting and composing your scene for the best rendering possible.

The art of rendering 3D images is closely related to the field of photography. In both cases, lights and cameras are used to set up a scene. Once the scene is composed, rendering the image is like snapping a picture.

To work with the concepts in this chapter, load 3D Studio now.

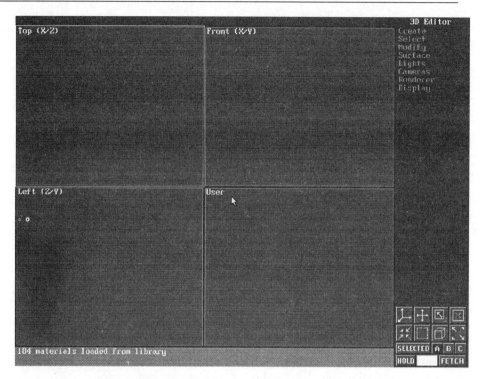

FIGURE 5-1. 3D Studio screen.

Import DXF File

To import a DXF file in 3D Studio, choose the *File* menu and choose *Load*. The file selector appears.

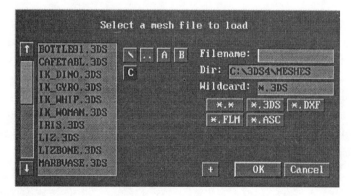

FIGURE 5-2. File selector.

Click on the *.DXF wildcard selector at the right of the screen. The file listing will change to show only DXF files. Select a DXF file.

The following dialog box appears.

This dialog box gives you a number of choices for DXF import.

Layer, Color, Entity. When the drawing is imported, this selection determines how objects will be delineated. In all our work so far, we have separated objects by layer. This is the method recommended by Autodesk, and the only method we will use in this book.

Weld Vertices. When two vertices in the drawing are very close together but not connected, they will be welded together if this option is set to Yes. The default selection Yes is the usual choice.

Unify Normals. When this choice is set to Yes, the DXF import filter does its best to make all surface normals point outward. The default selection Yes is the usual choice.

Auto-smooth and Smoothing angle. When **Auto-smooth** is set to Yes, the DXF import filter uses the **Smoothing angle** setting to determine which parts of objects will appear to be rounded and which will appear to have sharp edges.

The DXF import filter looks at the angle between two adjacent faces and checks it against the specified smoothing angle.

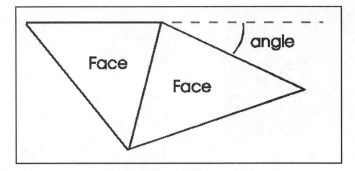

FIGURE 5-3. Angle between two faces.

If the angle is less than the Smoothing angle, the two faces will have a smooth surface between them. If the angle is larger than the smoothing angle, the two faces will appear to meet at a hard angle. See Figure 5-4.

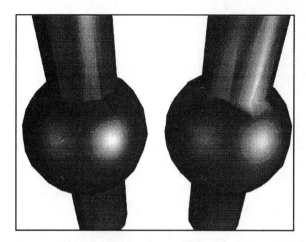

FIGURE 5-4. Object on the left has a smoothing angle of 30. Object on the right with smoothing angle of 80.

A Smoothing angle of 30 works for most models. Leave the smoothing angle at its default value of 30 unless you have a particular reason for changing it.

To try out the DXF import function, import the file OFFICE.DXF.

Locating Objects

During the DXF conversion process, all 3D entities on any one AutoCAD layer have been converted to an individual object. To see the list of objects, choose *Select/Object/By Name*. A list of objects appears.

FIGURE 5-5. Object name listing.

Look through the list to see the object names. Note that every layer is represented in the list as a separate object.

Locate the object FLOOR01 on the list. Click on the object name. An asterisk appears next to the object name.

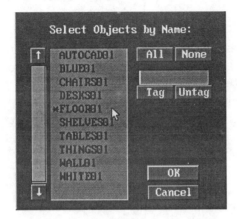

FIGURE 5-6. Object name listing with asterisk next to selected object.

Click on **OK**.

The FLOOR01 object has now turned red on the screen. When you select an object in 3D Studio, it turns red. This will not affect the rendering or any other aspect of the model. Selecting an object simply makes it easier to locate on the screen.

Now select other objects in the same way. As each object turns red you'll be able to see where it's located in the model.

You can also select objects to make them easier to manipulate. Selected objects can be moved or rotated as a group. Object selection is also useful when you have difficulty picking an object from the screen. The object can be selected by name, then you can manipulate just the selected object. A group of selected objects is called a *selection set*.

Selection in 3D Studio works differently than it does in AutoCAD. In AutoCAD you enter a command and it asks you to pick objects (entities). In 3D Studio you choose the selection set first, then choose the command you want to use. After choosing the command, click on the SELECTED button at the lower right of the screen. The command will now apply to all selected objects.

Creating Objects

After importing the model to 3D Studio you might find that you need a few additional objects. A very useful object is a *box*. In 3D Studio, a box is any six-sided object composed entirely with right angles. A box is very easy to make in 3D Studio, and can be used for walls, floors, window panes, the ground and many other architectural objects. To create a box you can either type in coordinates or draw the box interactively.

To draw a box with coordinates, choose the *Create/Box* menu option. Enter the X, Y and Z coordinates for one corner of the box, pressing ⏎ between each entry. Your entries will appear on the status line at the top of the screen. Enter second and third set of X, Y,

Z coordinates to define the box. 3D Studio will draw the box using the specified coordinates.

To draw a box interactively, choose the *Create/Box* menu option. Draw one side of the box in any viewport. To do this, move the cursor to the location of one corner of the box in any viewport. Click to set one corner, then move the cursor and click to set the opposite corner of the box. You now need to set the thickness of the box in the remaining direction. To do this, click once anywhere on the viewport, then move the cursor until the desired thickness is achieved. Watch the status line at the top of the screen to see the length of the line. Click to set the thickness. 3D Studio will draw the box on the construction plane.

The interactive method might seem haphazard to an AutoCAD user accustomed to exact coordinates, but this method is handy when coordinates are not known. Because boxes can be used for so many types of objects, you will find it useful to become proficient at creating them.

MATERIALS

3D Studio comes with a variety of premade materials. Many of these materials can be used as-is in an architectural rendering.

To see the list of premade materials, choose *Surface/Material/Choose*. The list of premade materials appears.

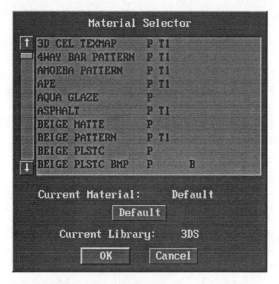

FIGURE 5-7. Materials listing.

Choose a material from the list. This material becomes the *current material*. Only one material can be current at any time.

The material can now be applied to an object. To apply a material, choose *Surface/Material/Assign/Object*. Click on an object on the screen.

The material has now been applied to the object. Once a material is assigned to an object, the material is saved with the geometry and need not be reapplied. It is impossible to tell if an object has a material applied to it just by looking at the wireframe. The material shows up only in the rendering.

Materials Editor

As you learned in Chapter 2, materials are made up of many components. Materials are created in the Materials Editor. To go to the Materials Editor, choose *Program/Materials Editor*. The Materials Editor appears.

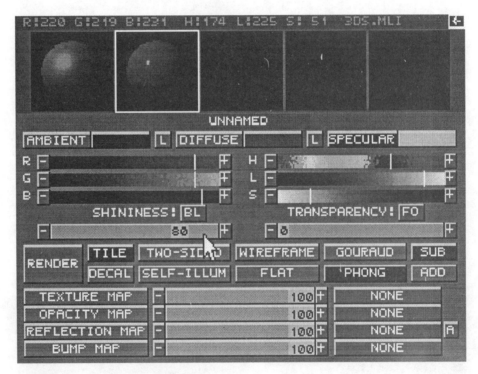

FIGURE 5-8. Materials Editor screen.

There are many settings on this screen. Not all of them are covered in this book. In this chapter and the chapters that follow, the settings that are used most often for architectural rendering will be covered.

Across the top of the screen are seven boxes. As you create a material you can view a sample rendering in one of these boxes.

As an example, load the material RED PLASTIC. To do this, choose the *Materials* pull-down menu and choose *Get Material*.

FIGURE 5-9. Material menu.

A list of materials appears. This is a list of materials that comes with 3D Studio. Move down the list until you find RED PLASTIC. Choose RED PLASTIC from the list.

After a few moments a red sphere will appear in the first box. Also note that the name RED PLASTIC appears just under the boxes. The red sphere gives you an idea of how the material RED PLASTIC will look when applied to an object.

Some of the settings also changed when you loaded the material RED PLASTIC. The color next to *Diffuse* has changed to red, and the *Shininess* slider has increased.

To see another material, click on the second box at the top of the screen. Choose the *Materials* pull-down menu and choose *Get Material*. Select another material. Note the appearance of the sample sphere and the changes to the settings.

Ambient, Diffuse, Specular

Just under the sample boxes you will find three color settings: Ambient, Diffuse and Specular.

FIGURE 5-10. Ambient, Diffuse, Specular.

The *Diffuse* color is the main color of the material. To make a material to simulate blue paint, for example, you'd make the Diffuse color blue.

The *Ambient* color is the color of the material when the object is in shadow or indirect lighting. The Ambient color has nothing to do with the Ambient light setting in the 3D Editor.

The *Specular* color is the color of the highlight on a shiny material.

To change the Ambient, Diffuse and Specular colors, click on the color label and use the RGB and HLS sliders.

RGB and HLS Sliders

The RGB and HLS sliders are used to change material colors interactively.

FIGURE 5-11. RGB and HLS sliders.

In Chapter 2 you learned about the Red/Green/Blue color wheel and the concepts of hue, luminance and saturation. The R, G and B sliders refer to the colors red, green and blue. The H, L and S sliders refer to hue, luminance and saturation.

To see how these sliders work, click on the **Diffuse** button if it is not already selected. Move the RGB or HLS sliders and watch how they affect the Diffuse color.

The Ambient and Specular colors can be changed in the same way. After you've changed the colors, render the sample sphere by clicking on the *Render* button at the lower left of the screen.

Shininess

A material is also defined by its shininess. The level of shininess is set with the *Shininess* slider.

You can see the effects of this slider by moving it left and right and rendering the sample sphere to see the effect. The slider must be set higher than zero in order to have a shiny material.

The Shininess slider affects the size of the highlight. The higher the Shininess setting, the smaller and brighter the highlight will be. The lower the setting, the larger and dimmer the highlight will be.

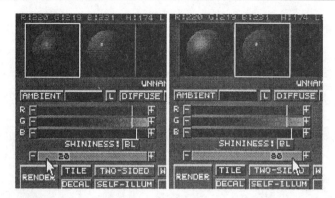

FIGURE 5-12. Spheres with Shininess 20 and 80.

Texture Map

A texture map is a bitmap applied like wallpaper to an object. When you assign a bitmap as a texture map, the bitmap is tiled all over the object.

To assign a bitmap as a texture map, click on the box labeled NONE across from the label *Texture*.

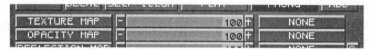

FIGURE 5-13. Texture map setting.

A file selector appears. Several bitmap files are listed. Choose one from the list. Render the sample sphere to see the effect of the texture map.

To see what the texture map looks like, choose the *Options* pull-down menu. Choose *View Image File*. Find the file you want to view. The image will appear. Press **ESC** to return to the Materials Editor.

The color of the object is determined by the bitmap in Texture map and the Diffuse color of the material. The slider next to **Texture** designates how intense the bitmap will appear on the object. For example, if Texture is set to 75 and the Diffuse color is blue, then the material will show the bitmap at a 75% intensity, filling in the remaining 25% with blue. If the value of the texture map is set to 100, the diffuse color makes no difference.

Naming a Material

Once a new material is made it must be named. When the word UNNAMED appears under the sample boxes, this indicates that the material is not yet named.

To name a material, choose the *Material* pull-down menu from the top of the screen. Choose *Put Material*.

FIGURE 5-14. Material menu.

Type in a material name and click on **OK**. The material name appears under the sample boxes in place of the word UNNAMED.

Premade Materials

3D Studio comes with a variety of premade architectural materials. For exteriors there are the materials BROWN BRICK, BUMPYWHITE STONE, and various MARBLEs and CHROMEs.

For interiors there are several materials that can be used for carpeting, wallpaper and upholstery. These materials can also be used as a base for building your own custom materials.

To access the premade materials, choose the *Material* menu. Select *Get Material*. The list of premade materials appears. Choose a material. The selected material will render in the current sample box.

To rename a premade material, choose *Material/Put Material* and type a new material name.

Materials Libraries

A material can be saved in a *materials library*. A materials library is a collection of materials saved in a file. A materials library file is saved in the Materials Editor and has the extension MLI.

When 3D Studio is loaded, the default materials library 3DS.MLI is loaded. The premade materials you looked at in the previous section are all saved in 3DS.MLI.

If you like, you can create your own materials libraries. A materials library containing only architectural materials can be useful for creating quick renderings of your models.

Assigning Materials to Objects

Materials are created in the Materials Editor, but are assigned to objects in the 3D Editor. In order to assign a material to an object it must be assigned as the *current material*.

Only one material can be the current material at any time. The current material can then be assigned to an object in the 3D Editor.

Before switching to the 3D Editor, any changes made to materials should be saved to the materials library. If you don't save changes to a library before ending your 3D Studio session, any changes you made to materials will be lost.

To save your work, first put each changed material to the library with *Material/Put Material*. When you name the material you put it to the library, but if any changes have been made to the material since it was named, this step must be performed again in order to save the changes. Then choose *Library/Save Library*. In the dialog box that appears, the name of your current materials library will be shown. Click on **OK** to save over this library. When asked if you want to overwrite the library, click on **OK**.

In general you will follow this sequence when creating and assigning materials:

- Go to the Materials Editor.
- Make a material, either by choosing a premade material and modifying it, or by creating a material from scratch.
- Put the material to the current materials library with *Material/Put Material.*
- Save the library with *Library/Save Library*.
- Go to the 3D Editor and choose *Surface/Material/Choose* to pick the material from the list.
- Choose *Surface/Material/Assign/Object* and click on an object to assign the material.

The diagram below illustrates how materials are created and assigned in 3D Studio.

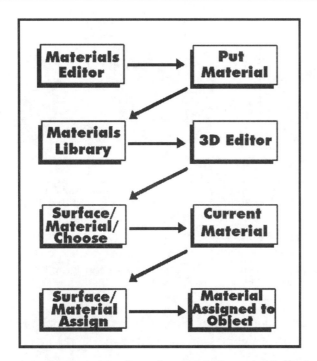

FIGURE 5-15. The flow of materials through 3D Studio.

MAPPING COORDINATES

When a bitmap is part of a material setup, you will need to apply *mapping coordinates* to any object holding that material. Mapping coordinates are a set of values that tell 3D Studio how to orient a material's bitmap on the object.

For example, suppose you have applied the material BROWN BRICK to a flat box. You must tell 3D Studio which face of the box the bitmap will lie upon.

FIGURE 5-16. Boxes with mapping on different face planes.

Planar mapping coordinates are represented graphically in 3D Studio as a 2D rectangular box. The plane of the box sets the mapping coordinates.

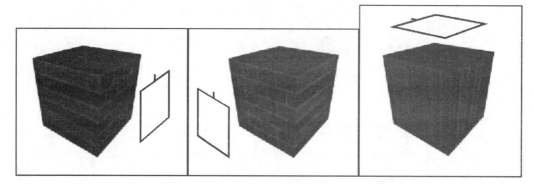

FIGURE 5-17. Mapping coordinates and corresponding mapped boxes.

Mapping coordinates are drawn and applied in the 3D Editor. The mapping coordinates box is defined as having an X and Y size. These terms are used when working with the two directions of the box, and have nothing to do with the global X and Y axes in 3D space.

Mapping coordinates determine not only the orientation of the bitmap but its size relative to the object. One iteration of the bitmap is placed in the XY box and tiled infinitely in both the X and Y directions.

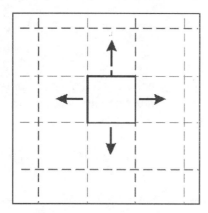

FIGURE 5-18. Mapping coordinates tile infintely in all directions.

Mapping coordinates have no Z depth. The bitmap, however, is "pushed" infinitely in the Z direction of the mapping coordinates.

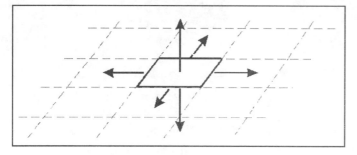

FIGURE 5-19. Mapping coordinates also tile infinitely in the Z direction.

This three-dimensional tiling means the sides of the object perpendicular to the mapping coordinates will have a "stretched" look. The stretched look, visible on the brick cube in Figure 5-18, is usually not a problem in practice. In most cases the edges of objects such as walls and floors will be hidden from view. However, when you see stripes on an object where a bitmap should be, this means the mapping coordinates are not at the correct orientation.

Applying Mapping Coordinates

The use of mapping coordinates with an object requires a two-step process: first you *set* the mapping coordinates, then you *apply* them to the object. The same mapping coordinates can be applied to many different objects.

Mapping coordinates can be set in many different ways. The easiest way is to choose *Surface/Mapping/Aspect/Region Fit*. This menu option allows you to draw the mapping coordinates at any size in any viewport you choose.

The choice of viewport is very important in drawing mapping coordinates. If you're making mapping coordinates for the floor, the Top viewport is the best choice. For a wall you should use the Front or Left viewport, whichever gives you a face-on view of the wall.

Once mapping coordinates are set, they must be *applied*. When you're drawing mapping coordinates, 3D Studio has no way of knowing which object they relate to. When you *apply* them to an object, you're linking the the current mapping coordinates to the object. Once mapping coordinates are applied they will "stick" to the object, and need not be applied again.

The following is a useful procedure for setting and applying mapping coordinates.

- Zoom in on object in the Top, Front and Left viewports.
- Choose *Surface/Mapping/Aspect/Region Fit*. Draw the mapping coordinates in the appropriate viewport.
- Choose *Surface/Mapping/Apply/Object*. Click on the appropriate object to apply the mapping coordinates.

It's easy to forget to *apply* the mapping coordinates once they've been defined. Remember that you must reapply the coordinates each time you change them. Otherwise 3D Studio has no way of knowing which object the changed coordinates refer to.

About Mapping Coordinates

Only one set of mapping coordinates is active at any time. As soon as you redraw the mapping coordinates you lose the previous settings. After mapping coordinates have been applied to an object, you can obtain them from the object at any time with *Surface/Mapping/Adjust/Acquire*.

When drawing mapping coordinates with *Region Fit*, you can restrict the XY box to a perfect square by holding down the **Ctrl** key while you draw.

Once mapping coordinates have been drawn, you can edit them with the options under *Surface/Mapping/Adjust*. For example, the *Rotate* option allows you to turn the mapping coordinates in any direction.

It is common to have two walls in a model that require mapping coordinates at 90 degrees to one another. If the walls are part of the same object, they must have the same mapping coordinates. You can get around this problem by applying mapping coordinates at 45 degrees to each wall.

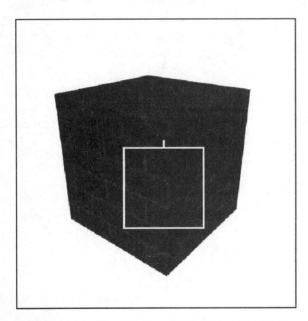

FIGURE 5-20. Mapping coordinates at a 45-degree angle to both walls.

To set up this kind of mapping, first draw the mapping coordinates in one viewport. Then use *Surface/Mapping/Adjust/Rotate* to turn the mapping coordinates by 45 degrees.

Rendering

If you have assigned a bitmap material to an object but have neglected to apply mapping coordinates to it, the following message will appear during rendering:

Object "WALL01" needs mapping coordinates.
Continue rendering?

If you choose to render under these circumstances, the renderer will shade the object with the Ambient, Diffuse and Specular colors rather than the bitmaps in the material.

LIGHTS

In order see your model in the rendering, lights must be placed in a scene. Three types of lights can be used in 3D Studio:

Omni Lights. An omni light shines in all directions from its source. Omni lights are useful for providing basic illumination. They also shine through objects, a feature which will be explored later on. Omni lights do not cast shadows.

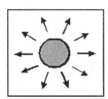

FIGURE 5-21. Omni lights shine in all directions.

Spotlights. A spot light shines from its source in a specific direction. Spotlights shine only over a specified area. They can cast shadows.

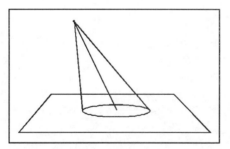

FIGURE 5-22. Spotlights shine over a specified area.

Ambient light. Ambient light is overall lighting applied uniformly to the model. It can be likened to twilight, where shadows and highlights disappear and the world seems to be lit in a uniform dim gray. Ambient light has nothing to do with the Ambient color setting in the Materials Editor.

Light Intensity

Lights are set with a color slider. When you choose *Lights/Omni/Create*, *Lights/Spot/Create* or *Lights/Ambient* a color slider appears:

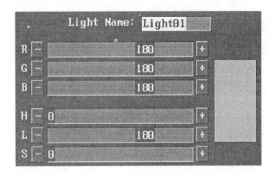

FIGURE 5-23. Lights color slider.

Although lights can be any color, gray or white lights work best for architectural rendering. Colored lights are used mainly for "mood" lighting and special effects. To set up a gray/white light you need only move the *Luminance* (L) slider in the color dialog box.

A scene usually needs more than one light. For the best effect, give each light a different Luminance value. In general, one light should be quite bright with a Luminance value of 180-255. This light will provide the main lighting for the scene. Other dimmer lights with Luminance of 50-100 can provide additional illumination.

Add up all the Luminance values as you go along. In your initial setup the total Luminance should be between 250 and 500. This will prevent you from over or underlighting your scene. A poorly lit scene results in low contrast and pale colors.

You may find after a test rendering that the model needs more lighting. In this case it's fine to increase the luminance of the lights. The total value of 500 is a "Rule of Thumb" and need not be slavishly followed, but it is useful for an initial lighting setup. A common beginner's mistake try to compensate for a low-contrast scene by adjusting materials. The only solution for this problem is to lower or raise the overall Luminance of individual lights.

Omni Lights

Omni Lights shine in all directions. Omni lights also shine through objects. See Figure 5-24.

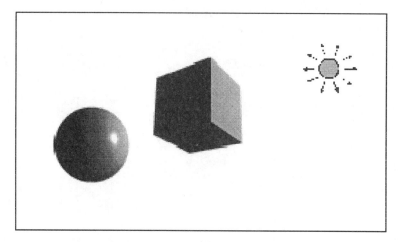

FIGURE 5-24. The omni light shines through the cube to the sphere.

Just because omni lights shine through objects does not mean the entire object is illuminated. An omni light illuminates all faces in the scene where the normals point toward the omni light's rays. In the figure above, the sphere is behind the cube, but the omni light's rays still reach it. However, only the parts of the sphere facing the omni light's rays are illuminated.

Because they shine in all directions and also shine through objects, omni lights are useful for general illumination in a scene. To change the Luminance of an omni light, choose *Lights/Omni/Adjust* and click on the light.

Spotlights

Spotlights shine in one direction, and only over a specified area. The endpoint of a spotlight is called the spotlight *target*.

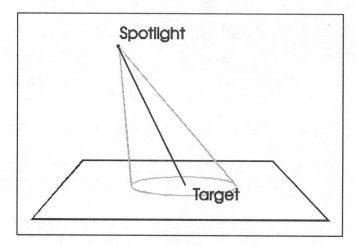

FIGURE 5-25. Spotlight and target.

The direction of the target is important while its location is not. A spotlight will shine infinitely in the direction of the target.

You can also set the sharpness or fuzziness of the spotlight edge with the *hotspot* and *falloff* settings. The hotspot delimits the area where the light will shine at full strength. The falloff determines where the spotlight ceases to shine. The falloff is always larger than the hotspot.

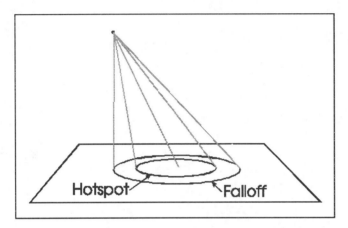

FIGURE 5-26. Spotlight hotspot and falloff.

The area between the hotspot and falloff gradually fades from full strength to no strength. A wide difference between hotspot and falloff makes a fuzzy spotlight edge. If the hotspot and falloff are nearly the same, the spotlight edge will be sharp. See Figure 5-27.

FIGURE 5-27. The spotlight on the left has a large difference between hotspot and falloff. The spotlight on the right has nearly the same hotspot and falloff.

The hotspot and falloff can be changed interactively with the *Lights/Spot/Hotspot* and *Lights/Spot/Falloff* menu options.

A spotlight can also cast shadows, while omni lights cannot. Shadows are discussed in more detail in *Chapter 7*.

To change the Luminance or turn on shadows after a spotlight has been created, choose *Lights/Spot/Adjust* and click on the light.

3D Studio beginners often want to use only spotlights and avoid omni lights altogether. The problem with this method is that spotlights, when used incorrectly, do not sufficiently illuminate a scene. The inexperienced user then adds more badly-placed spotlights in an attempt to fix the problem, and rendering time slows to a crawl while the image quality doesn't improve.

It's ridiculous to waste your time with improperly placed spotlights. Your work will go faster if you light the scene with omni lights at first so you can see the objects and materials clearly. Once all your objects and materials have been adjusted to your satisfaction, you can then replace the omni lights with spotlights.

Ambient Light

If a scene is dark, you may be tempted to simply increase Luminance of the Ambient light. This is usually not a good idea. When you increase the ambient light, the entire scene becomes lighter but contrast is greatly decreased. A high ambient light level loses the perpective effect -- all objects look as if they're the same distance from the camera. Strong ambient light also makes it difficult to distinguish one object from another.

The Ambient light Luminance value defaults to 77. You will probably not want to increase this value, and would more likely improve a scene by lowering it.

Placing Lights

In general, lights should be placed well away from the focus of the scene. This rule makes sense when you consider light placement in real life. In a building interior, lights are near the ceiling. In an exterior scene, the main light is the sun.

In 3D Studio, a light placed relatively far away from the model will illuminate more objects, saving you the trouble of placing multiple lights. Remember that the more lights you place, the more difficult it will be to make adjustments to the scene.

Placing lights is a two-step process. First you create the lights in one viewport, usually the Top viewport. When you look in the Front and Left viewports you will usually find that the lights are not at the appropriate height. The lights must then be moved in the Front or Left viewports.

To place lights, follow this procedure:

- Right-click on **Zoom Extents** to view the entire model in all viewports. If necessary, zoom out a few times to make room for the light.
- Choose *Lights/Omni/Create* or *Lights/Spot/Create*. In the Top viewport, place the light at the appropriate location in relation to the model.
- Choose *Lights/Omni/Move* or *Lights/Spot/Move*. Move the light and/or target in the Front and Left viewports.

Camera

A camera provides a perspective view of your model. A camera can be placed anywhere in or around a model to view it from any angle. A 3D Studio camera can also simulate a zoom or wide angle lens for a variety of effects.

The direction in which the camera looks is determined by its *target*. A camera is defined by both its camera and target positions.

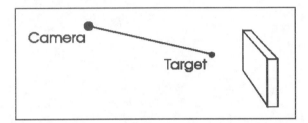

FIGURE 5-28. Camera and target.

The direction of the target is more important than its position. A camera sees the model infinitely in the target direction.

To create a camera, choose *Cameras/Create*. Click to set the camera, then click to set the target. The camera dialog box appears.

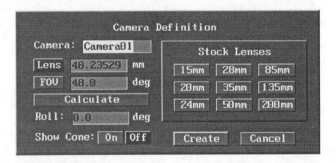

In most cases the default values are the most desirable camera settings. Click on **Create** to set the camera. A small blue icon appears on the screen to show the camera and target positions. When placing a camera, follow this procedure:

- Right-click on **Zoom Extents** to view the entire model in all viewports. If necessary, zoom out a few times to make room for the camera.
- Choose *Cameras/Create*. Place the camera and target in the Top viewport.
- Put the camera view in the lower right viewport. To do this, click on the lower right viewport to select it, then press the **C** key on the keyboard. the lower right view changes to the camera view.
- Choose *Cameras/Move*. Move the camera and target in the Front, Left and Top viewports until you are satisfied with the camera view.

When cameras are created, 3D Studio places them on the construction plane.

Rendering

Once cameras, lights and materials have been set up you can render the image. To render the model, choose *Renderer/Render*. Click on the camera viewport. If the camera viewport is not the current viewport, you will have to click twice.

The Render Still Image dialog box appears.

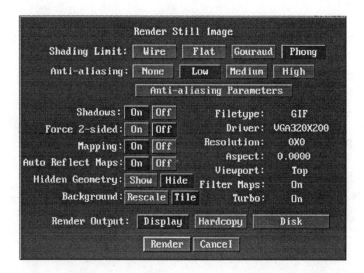

In most cases the default settings will work fine, and you can click on **Render** without any further ado.

In some cases you will want to change the default settings. It's a good idea to become familiar with the rendering options so you can change them when necessary. A full description of rendering options can be found in the *3D Studio Reference Manual*.

The buttons you will be most concerned with are:

Force 2-Sided. When this option is turned on, both sides of each face in the model will be rendered. A model imported from AutoCAD sometimes contains faces on which the normals are pointing the wrong way. This will cause the model to appear to have "holes" in it in the rendering. Turning this option on forces both sides of each face to be rendered, getting rid of the holes in the rendering.

Shadows. Turns shadows on and off. When performing test renderings, you can turn shadows off to make the image render faster. Be sure to turn shadows back on when you want the shadows to appear again.

Disk. When turned on, the rendering will be saved to a disk file. The file format is determined by the settings under the Configure option. When Disk is turned on, a file selector appears. Enter the name of the file, then click on OK to begin rendering.

Try not to confuse the *Renderer/Render* and *Renderer/View/Image* commands. The first command renders an image, while the latter displays a previously saved rendering.

SUMMARY

In general, your work in 3D Studio will follow this sequence:

- Import the DXF model.
- Place lights.
- Place a camera. Change the lower right viewport to the camera view.
- Make and assign materials.
- Apply mapping coordinates.
- Render the camera view.

Once you have rendered the model, you can check the rendering and adjust lights and materials accordingly.

The 3D Studio file can be saved as either a 3DS file with *File/Save*, or as a project file with *File/Save Project*.

TUTORIALS

Tutorial 1

1. Import file

Import the house you made with the Tutorial in Chapter 4. To do this, go to the 3D Editor and choose *File/Load*. Click on the *.DXF file selector. Locate the subdirectory that holds the file **3DHOUSE.DXF**. Click on the file to import it.

When the import dialog box appears, accept all the defaults. The house model appears on the screen in all four viewports.

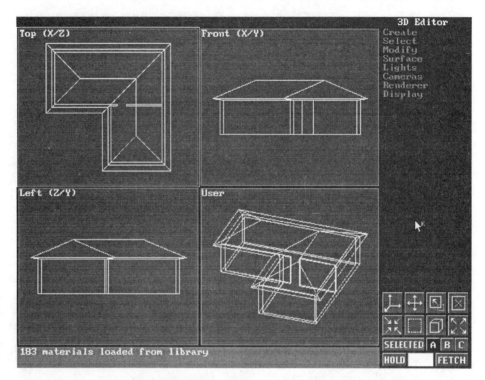

FIGURE 5-29. House model in 3D Studio.

2. Create Ground Plane

The house is sitting in space. To make a ground plane you'll create a flat box.

Right-click on **Zoom Out** three times to give yourself room to make the ground plane. Choose *Create/Box*. In the Top viewport, draw a box that encompasses the model, as shown in Figure 5-31.

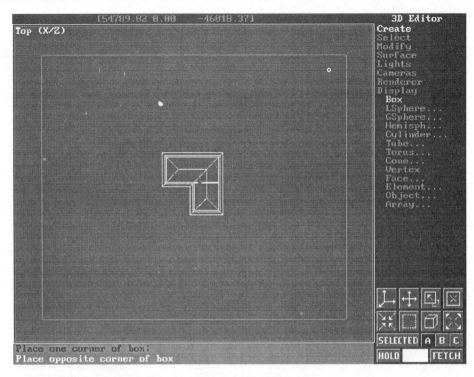

FIGURE 5-30. Ground plane drawn in Top viewport.

After the box has been drawn, click in the Front viewport to define the length of the box. The box does not have to be very high. See Figure 5-32.

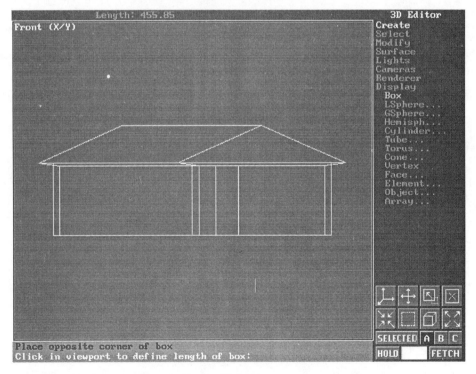

FIGURE 5-31. Length of box in Front viewport.

Call the object **Ground**. When you click on **Create**, the box will appear in all four viewports.

Because of the location of the construction plane, the box has ended up too high on the Y axis. You must move the box. First, zoom in on the corner of the house in the front viewport with **Zoom Window**, as shown in Figure 5-33.

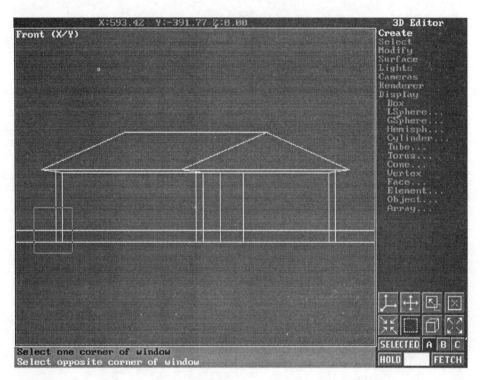

FIGURE 5-32. Zoom in on corner of house.

Choose *Modify/Object/Move*. Move the cursor to the Front viewport. Press the TAB key until the up-down arrow appears. Click on the box and move it down until the top of the box sits just below the bottom of the house.

If you are having difficulty telling where the bottom of the house is, you can zoom in further. You can also use *Views/Redraw* to redraw the screen if parts of the house are erased during the moving process.

When you're finished, the ground plane should sit just below the house, as shown in Figure 5-33.

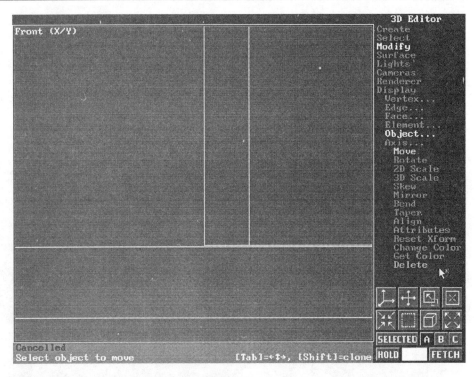

FIGURE 5-33. Ground plane below house.

Right-click on Zoom Extents to see the ground plane in all four viewports.

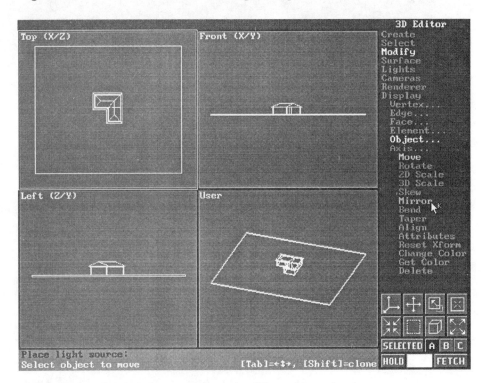

FIGURE 5-34. Ground plane and house in all four viewports.

3. Place Lights

To place lights to the scene, choose *Lights/Omni/Create*. Click at the lower right corner of the Top viewport to set the first light.

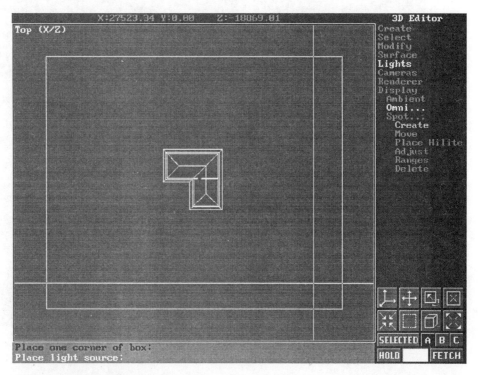

FIGURE 5-35. Light placement.

When the Light Definition dialog box appears, move the Luminance (L) slider to 200. This light will be the main source of illumination.

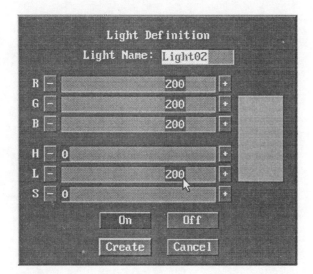

FIGURE 5-36. Light luminance value changed to 200.

Place two more lights in the Top viewport. Place one at the lower left of the screen with a Luminance of 150, and another light at the top of the viewport with a Luminance of 50.

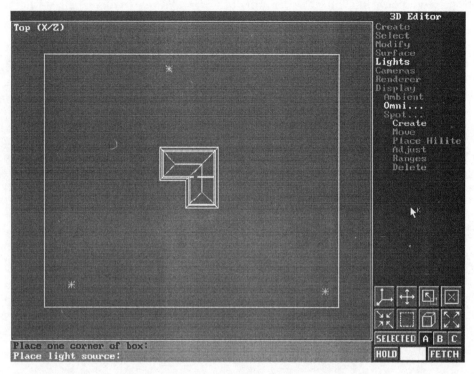

FIGURE 5-37. Light placement in Top viewport.

In the Front and Left viewports you can see that the lights are too low -- they're sitting on the ground plane. Move the lights by choosing *Lights/Omni/Move*. In the Front or Left viewports, move the lights upward so they sit above the house, as shown in Figure 5-38.

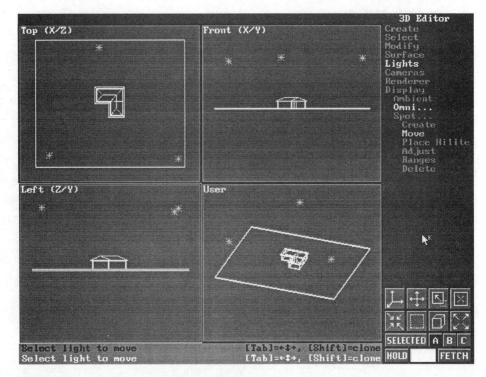

FIGURE 5-38. Light placement in all viewports.

4. Place Camera

To place the camera, choose *Cameras/Create*. Click in the Top viewport to select the viewport. Place the camera in the Top viewport as shown below. Click once to set the camera and again to set the target.

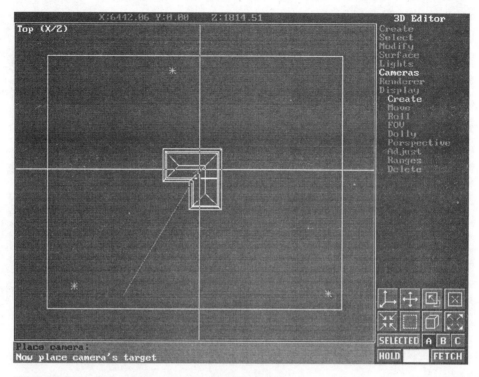

FIGURE 5-39. Camera placement in Top viewport.

When the Camera Definition dialog box appears, accept the default values and click on **Create**.

Click on the User viewport. Press the **C** key. The camera view appears in the viewport.

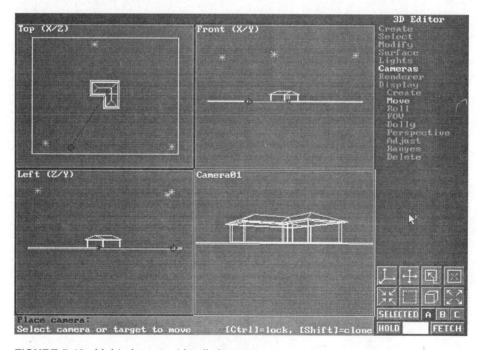

FIGURE 5-40. Light placement in all viewports.

The camera is too low. Choose *Cameras/Move* and move the camera in the Front or Left viewports.

If the house is not centered in the Camera viewport, move the target rather than the camera. To move the target, choose *Cameras/Move* and click on the target.

Work with the camera and target until your view resembles the view shown below.

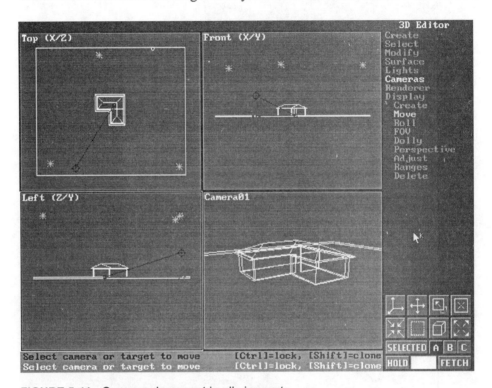

FIGURE 5-41. Camera placement in all viewports.

5. Assign Material

For a quick and easy rendering, assign the material RED MATTE to the entire scene. To do this, choose *Surface/Material/Choose*. Find the material RED MATTE on the list, and select it.

Choose *Surface/Material/Assign/By Name*. Click on All to assign the material RED MATTE to all objects. Click on **OK**.

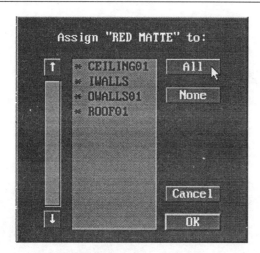

FIGURE 5-42. Material assignment.

The material RED MATTE has now been assigned to all objects in the scene.

5. Render

Choose Renderer/Render View. Click twice on the camera viewport. The Render Still Image dialog box appears. Click on Disk if you want to save the rendering. Click on Render.

After a few moments, the rendered image will appear.

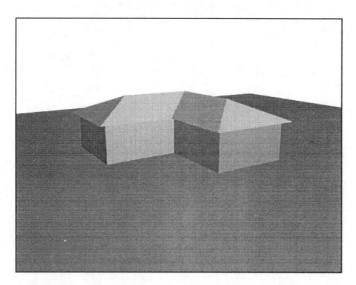

FIGURE 5-43. Rendered house.

After viewing rendering, press ESCAPE to return to 3D Editor.

Save the file as 3DHOUSE.3DS.

Tutorial 2

In this tutorial you'll assign the material MARBLE - PALE to the house walls, and WHITE MATTE to the ceiling. MARBLE - PALE requires mapping coordinates. For this reason, you'll also assign 45 degree mapping coordinates to the walls of the house.

1. Assign materials

Choose *Surface/Material/Choose*. Select the material MARBLE - PALE.

Choose *Surface/Material/Assign/By Name*. Select the objects IWALL01 and OWALL01. These objects represent the inner and outer walls. This will assign the material MARBLE - PALE to these objects.

Choose *Surface/Material/Choose*. Select the material WHITE MATTE. Choose *Surface/Material/Assign/By Name*. Select the object CEILING.

2. Apply Mapping Coordinates

Choose *Surface/Mapping/Adjust/Region Fit*. In the Front viewport, draw mapping coordinates at approximately the size shown. Draw the icon from top left to lower right to orient it properly.

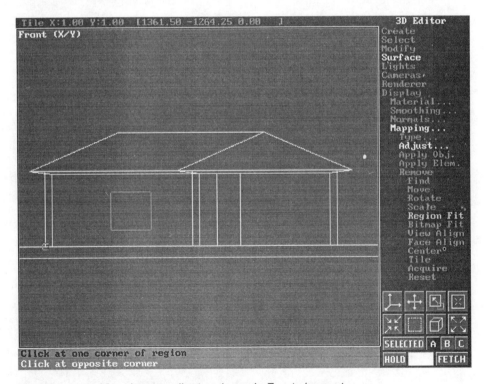

FIGURE 5-44. Mapping coordinates drawn in Front viewport.

Choose *Surface/Mapping/Adjust/Rotate*. In the Top viewport, rotate the mapping coordinates by 45 degrees. You may not be able to see the mapping coordinates as you rotate them. You must watch the top of the screen to see the current rotation angle.

To apply the mapping coordinates to the walls, choose *Surface/Mapping/Apply Object*. Press the **H** key. Choose IWALL01 from the list. Click on **OK**.

Press **H** again, and choose OWALL01 from the list. Click on **OK**. The mapping coordinates have now been applied to the walls.

3. Render

Choose *Renderer/Render* and click twice on the camera viewport. The Render Still Image dialog box appears. Click on **Disk** if you want to save the rendering. Click on **Render** to start rendering.

If you get the following message:

Object "IWALL01" needs mapping coordinates.
Continue rendering?

Then you have not properly assigned mapping coordinates to the walls. Repeat step 2 and try rendering again.

Once rendering looks correct, save it to project file 3DHOUSE.PRJ.

EXERCISE

Import the DXF file EXTRUDED.DXF which you made in *Exercise 1, Chapter 4*. When the file has been imported:

- Add a ground plane to the scene.
- Add two omni lights to the scene. Move the omni lights so they are well away from the objects as seen from the Top viewport. Also move the lights so they are above the objects in the Front viewport.
- Place a camera in the scene. Make the lower right viewport the camera view.
- Assign various materials to the objects in the scene. Apply mapping coordinates where necessary.
- Render the scene.

CHAPTER

6

3D STUDIO ANIMATION

Once you've set up a 3D Studio with lights, camera and materials, you're ready to fly your viewer around the model.

What is Animation?

Animation works with the same concept as film or video. A series of still images is played very quickly, fooling the viewer into thinking he sees motion. With 3D Studio, several still images are rendered and played back either on the computer screen or on video. One image in an animated sequence is called a *frame*.

What is the Keyframer?

3D Studio uses the concept of *keyframes*. This term comes from the field of hand-drawn animation. In organizing a project at a traditional animation studio, the director assigns senior animators the task of drawing the important frames to define the characters' motion and establish the flow of the sequence. For example, a senior animator might draw every 15th frame in a sequence. These establishing frames are called *keyframes*. The senior animator then gives the keyframes to a junior animator who proceeds to draw all the frames in between.

With 3D Studio, you're the senior animator. The Keyframer allows you to set up keyframes at any intervals you choose. The Keyframer then becomes the junior animator, filling in all the frames between your keyframes.

This approach makes 3D animation easy to produce. You can place a camera at the first frame, then simply move it to another location on the 50th frame. 3D Studio will create the animation for you, moving the camera smoothly from one position to the other over the 50 frames.

Frame Rate

In order for animation to play smoothly, it must play at a rate of at least 15 frames per second. Video animation plays at 30 frames per second. An onscreen presentation, 15 frames per second is an acceptable speed. At lower speeds the motion can appear "jerky" which is irritating for the viewer.

Animation Files

For onscreen playback, an animated sequence can be rendered to a flic. A flic is an 8-bit animation file with the extension FLI or FLC. This file format was developed by Autodesk specifically for onscreen playback. Use this format for the exercises in this book. A 320x200 flic is saved with the extension FLI; any other resolution is saved with the extension FLC.

For video playback the sequence is rendered to a series of individual 24-bit files. Specialized video equipment is required to view a 24-bit animated sequence.

Even if you plan to record animation to video, it's a good idea to perform test renderings to flic format. Flics take much less time to render than 24-bit files and can be played right on the computer screen.

When a flic has a high resolution such as 800x600, the computer sometimes cannot refresh the screen quickly enough to fool the eye. Even though you may have set up 3D Studio to play back at 15 frames per second, the limitations of your computer and video card may cause it to fall back to 5 or 10 frames per second.

In the Keyframer

Go to the Keyframer. To do this, pull down the *Program* menu and choose *Keyframer*.

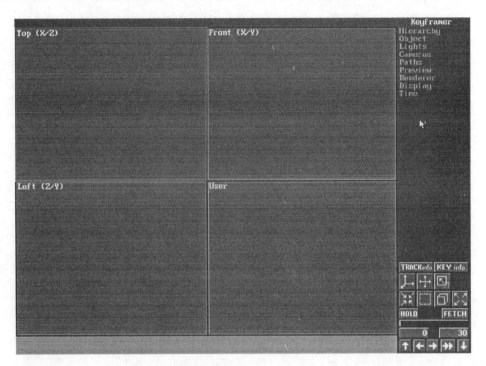

FIGURE 6-1. Keyframer screen.

The Keyframer resembles the 3D Editor. The main difference is that the Keyframer contains options especially for animation.

To see how the Keyframer works, load a file that already contains animation information. Choose *File/Load* and select the file BIRDWALK.3DS. This file shows a bird walking in front of a fence.

When the file has loaded, move your cursor to the bottom of the screen. A slider appears with a small box labeled 0 at the far left.

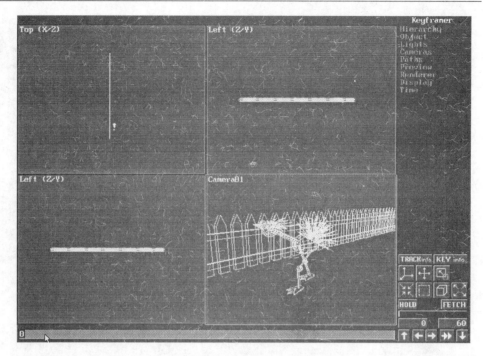

FIGURE 6-2. Keyframer screen with frame slider at bottom.

This slider shows the current frame, which is frame 0. The Keyframer numbers all frames starting with 0. Frame 0 is copy of the scene as it appears in the 3D Editor.

To change to another frame, click and drag the 0 box to the right. The number changes as you drag the box. Note that the model changes as well.

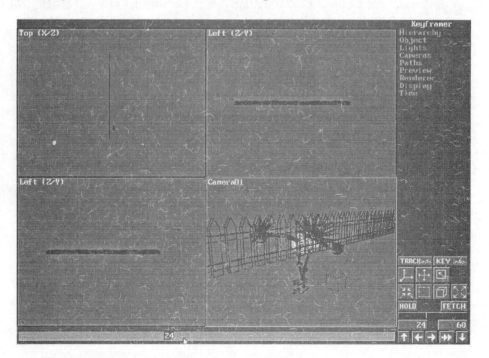

FIGURE 6-3. Frame 24 of animation.

The new number shows the number of the current frame. In the example above, we have moved to frame 24. The model has been changed on this frame to reflect what the animator wanted the bird to do on frame 24.

In the Keyframer, only one frame is current at any time. To create animation you simply move to a frame and manipulate the objects, lights or camera as desired on that frame. Objects can be changed with the *Objects/Move* option. Cameras are moved with *Cameras/Move* while lights are moved with *Lights/Move*. Most architectural work calls for animation of cameras and objects, but not lights.

At the lower right of the screen are two numbers. The first shows the current frame number; the second shows the total number of frames.

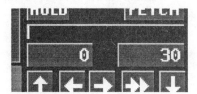

FIGURE 6-4. Current frame number and total number of frames in lower right corner of screen.

You can move to a particular frame by clicking on the current frame number and changing the number. Note that this achieves the same result as moving the slider at the bottom of the screen.

You can change the total number of frames by clicking on the total number of frames at the lower right of the screen. You can also change the total number of frames with the *Time/Total Frames* menu option.

At the lower right of the screen you will find several icons similar to those found on a videotape player.

FIGURE 6-5. Player icons.

⬆ Go to first frame.

⬅ Go to previous frame.

➡ Go to next frame.

⏩ Play wireframe animation.

⬇ Go to last frame.

Designing Animation

Before using the Keyframer you should do a little preparation. When you work out the keyframes ahead of time, the actual work in the Keyframer becomes very easy.

Grab a pencil and paper for the preparation. First, imagine the animation in your mind's eye and count out the seconds in the animation. Don't be concerned that this number might not be perfectly accurate. The estimated length is simply a starting point for your work, and can be changed later if necessary.

Next, multiply the length in seconds by your desired frame rate to get the total number of frames. For onscreen playback, use a frame rate of 15 frames/second. For video, use the standard video frame rate of 30 frames/second. For example, a 20-second animation for onscreen playback will require 20x15=300 frames. When you've calculated the total number of frames, write this number on your sheet of paper.

Next, sketch a simple plan view of the model on paper. Draw the path you'd like the camera to take through your model, and estimate how much time each movement will take. A sample drawing is shown below.

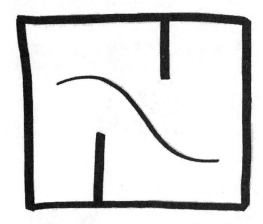

FIGURE 6-6. Sample plan.

Next, draw dots along the path, just enough to define the line. If you've worked with Bezier curves or splines you know that just a few points are necessary to define a curved line. The Keyframer works with curves as well, so only a few points are necessary to define a camera or object path.

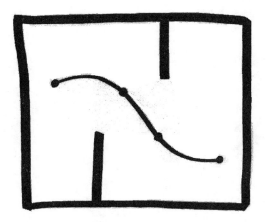

FIGURE 6-7. Dots to define path curve.

The dots you draw on the line will represent the camera positions at the various keyframes. The beginning and the end of the line are always keyframes. In the drawing above, four key positions are required to define the camera path. In your planning use the minimum number of points possible. If you're not sure about where to place the points, take an educated guess for now. As you become more experienced with the Keyframer you will develop a sense for where key points should be placed.

After you place the dots, also draw a line from each dot representing the camera target at that point. The camera target must be animated in the Keyframer along with the camera.

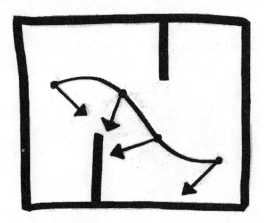

FIGURE 6-8. Arrows designating camera direction.

Now assign a keyframe number to each dot based on the length of each part of the animation. In the example below, the 300-frame animation has keyframes at frames 0, 100, 200 and 300.

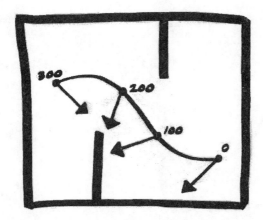

FIGURE 6-9. Path dots labeled with keyframe numbers.

Now that the key frames and camera positions have been worked out, it's a simple matter to go to the Keyframer, set the total number of frames, then move to each key frame and set the camera and target.

When first working with animation it's a good idea to keep the key positions at regular intervals. This will make it easier to determine the appropriate key frame numbers for each position. As you become more experienced you will be able to "speed up" and "slow down" the animation by changing the key frame numbers.

Camera Path

When moving the camera you can make your work easier by displaying the camera's path. To do this, choose *Paths/Show-Hide* and click on the camera. A yellow line with red dots appears on the screen.

FIGURE 6-10. Camera path.

This line represents the camera's path over the animation. Keyframes are denoted as white dots. You can move any keyframe on a path with the *Paths/Move Key* command.

Note that moving path keys is the only way to change a keyframe without actually being on that frame. Paths can also be displayed for objects, lights and the camera target.

Preview

Before rendering you can create a preview of your animated sequence. A preview is a quick grayscale rendering of an animation, usually created at a low resolution for fast rendering and playback.

To create a preview of an animation, choose *Preview/Make*. Click on the camera viewport once or twice. The Preview dialog box appears.

```
                        Make Preview
Draw:  [Faces][Faces+Lines][Lines]  Numbers:[No][Yes]

Hidden Face Accuracy:[Low][High]  Two-sided[No][Yes]

Frames:[All][Segment][Single]  Range:[0]  To:[29]
              Every Nth frame:[1]

Size:[320] by [200]  [320x200][200x125][160x100][108x80]
            [Preview]      [Cancel]
```

FIGURE 6-11. Make Preview dialog box.

You have several choices of resolution for the preview. Most often you can use the default settings. Click on **Preview** to start making the preview.

You will see each frame rendered quickly in succession. When all the frames have been rendered, the preview will play automatically, and will repeat until the **ESC** key is pressed. The action can be paused and resumed with the spacebar.

When you change some aspect of the animation you must make a new preview in order to see the changes. In some cases you might want to set **Numbers** to **Yes**. This displays the frame number in the top left corner of the preview, which can be handy for spotting and fixing errors in the animation.

Note that the preview function is primarily for checking motion. Shadows, materials and other subtleties are not rendered in a preview.

Track Info

If you later find that a keyframe setting should be moved to another frame, you can use Track Info to change it. Track Info gives you a graphical representation of your keyframes with an easy way to move them around.

To see Track Info for a camera, light or object, click on the Track Info button at the lower right of the screen, then click on the camera, light or object. The Track Info dialog box appears.

FIGURE 6-12. Track Info button.

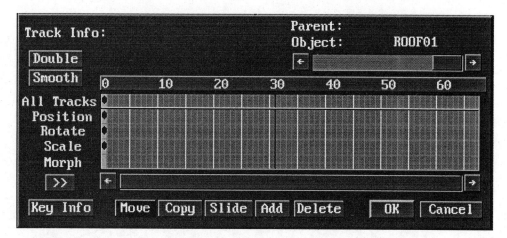

FIGURE 6-13. Track Info dialog box.

The camera, light or object name appears at the upper right of the box. Down the left side, each kind of key for the selected item appears. The slider at the upper right controls the object for which Track Info is displayed.

Frame numbers appear across the top of the box. A dot appears under each frame where a keyframe occurs. The dot is across from the key type that describes how the item was changed on that key.

For example, if you change the camera position on frame 25, a dot will appear under the number **25** across from **Position**.

If you want to change a keyframe to another frame, you can use the Move function on the Track Info box. Click on the **Move** button, then click on the dot to pick it up. Move the dot to another frame and click to set it down.

You can also use Track Info to make an animation loop seamlessly. This is accomplished by copying all the keyframe dots from frame 0 to the last frame of the animation. To do this, click on the **Copy** button. Click on the dot next to **All** under frame **0**. Move the dots to the last frame of animation, and click to set the keyframes. The animation on frame 0 has now been copied to the last frame of the animation.

You can see the tracks for other objects by moving the slider under the object name. If you move the slider all the way to the left you will see the object name **World**. This display, which represents all tracks for all objects, is useful for copying all tracks from frame 0 to the last frame for making all the motion loop. You can also see the **World** tracks by right-clicking on Track Info when it is first selected.

When you have finished working with the Track Info box, click on **OK** to set the changes. The screen will redraw to reflect the new information.

Rendering

After you have previewed the animation and are satisfied with the motion, it's time to render the animation.

The renderer needs to be configured. Choose *Renderer/Setup/Configure*. In the Device Configuration dialog box, choose settings for file output and resolution.

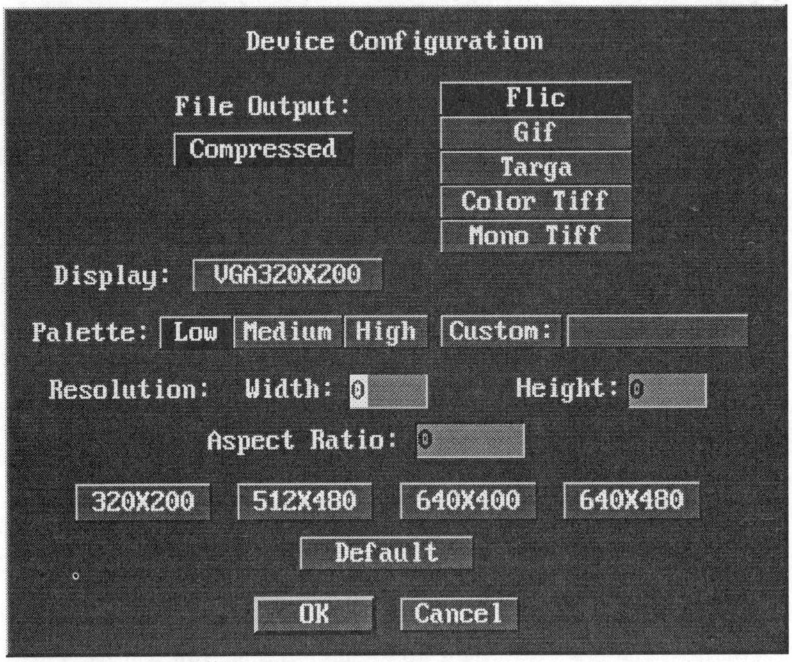

FIGURE 6-14. Device configuration dialog box.

The upper right of the dialog box gives you several output choices. For onscreen presentations, choose Flic. For video output you may want to use one of the other file types. Check with the manual that comes with your video equipment for the best file type choice.

You also have the choice of four preset resolutions. For onscreen presentations, 640x480 is recommended. This resolution provides sharp, clean images and smooth playback. A lower resolution such as 320x200 can appear grainy, while a higher resolution such as 800x600 may play back too slowly.

For video output, consult the video equipment manual for the recommended resolution.

Once you have chosen a file format and resolution, click on **OK** to exit this dialog box and return to the Render Animation dialog box.

To render, choose *Renderer/Render* and click on the camera view. The Render Animation dialog box appears.

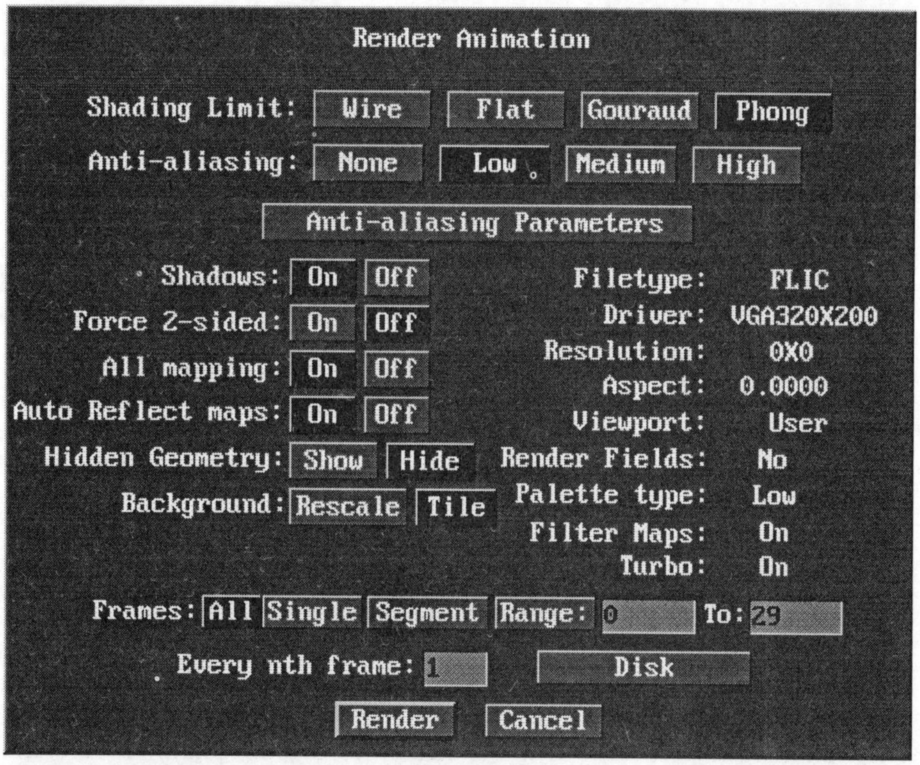

FIGURE 6-15. Render Animation dialog box.

The first setting in the Render Animation dialogue box is **Shading Limit** with the choices **Wire**, **Flat**, **Gouraud** and **Phong**. The shading limit controls the realism of the rendered image, and is related to the complexity of the model and materials. Simple geometry with simple materials applied would call for Flat or Gouraud shading. Flat shading applies one hue of a color across each face of the geometry. Gouraud shading adds the realism of a gradient of hues across the faces of geometry. Phong shading adds the further realism of shadows and complex mapped materials to the rendering. Each higher level of shading requires additional rendering time.

Below the shading limits is the Anti-aliasing setting. Aliasing refers to the jagged appearance of curves and diagonal lines in the rendering. For test renderings, set anti-aliasing to low, and set it to high for final renderings.

Similarly, shadows are generally turned off for test renderings.

Force 2-sided renders materials to both sides of every face, and is most often used to overcome problems with face normals, when incorrectly oriented faces are leaving holes in objects.

If the materials in the scene incorporate mapping, turn **Mapping** on.

The other setting you may want to change is the **Frames** setting. If you only want to render a segment of the animation, choose **Range**, and indicate a starting and ending frame. A common stategy for test renderings is to set **Every Nth Frame** to 2. A flic file with an FLI or FLC extension will be created from every other frame of the animation, which cuts rendering time in half.

You also might want to render a range of frames instead of the entire animation. In this case, click on the **Range** button and enter the range of frames.

It is also necessary to turn on the **Disk** button. This option will save the rendered animation to disk. You can play back the animation later only if it was rendered to disk.

Click on **Render**. A file selector appears. Enter a filename. In the case of multiple files such as those used in video output, the rendered files will be numbered. The first four characters of the name you enter will be used as the beginning of each filename, while a number will make up the remainder. For example, entering a filename BIRDWALK will yield the files BIRD0000.TGA, BIRD0001.TGA etc.

For flics, the entire animation is saved as one file. The entire filename you enter will be used, plus the extension FLC or FLI.

When rendering Flics, be sure that the **Disk** button is highlighted. When you click on **Render**, the Save Rendered Animation to File dialog box appears. Click on **OK** to start the rendering process. If the animation is not saved to your hard disk, it will not be viewable after it is rendered. In fact, the file will not exist at all. You must tell the renderer to write the file to disk.

When rendering begins, the Rendering status box appears. Wait until the first frame renders. Look at the time next to Last Frame Time. This time, multiplied by the total number of frames, will give you an idea of how long it will take to render the entire animation.

Playing Animation

Flic files can be played onscreen from within the Keyframer.

- Choose *Renderer/View/Flic*. A file selector appears.
- Choose a flic file to view. The flic will play on the screen. When the flic has played through, it will repeat.
- Press ESC to stop the flic and return to the Keyframer.

To set the speed of animation playback in 3D Studio, *choose Preview/Set Speed*. Change the speed to the desired frame rate, then view the flic. The speed can also be changed while the animation is playing by pressing the left and right arrow keys on the keyboard. The left arrow key slows down the animation playback speed while the right arrow key speeds it up.

Using the Keyframer

In creating an animated sequence, your work will usually follow this sequence:

Task	Keyframer Command
Design the animation with pencil and paper.	
Import or create a model in 3D Studio. Assign materials, lights and a camera.	
Go to the Keyframer.	*Program/Keyframer*
Move to each keyframe. Move the camera and camera target to the appropriate position.	*Cameras/Move, Paths/Show-Hide*
Preview the animation.	*Preview/Make*
Make any necessary changes to the animation.	Track Info, *Cameras/Move*
Render the animation.	*Renderer/Render View*

TABLE 6-16. Animation tasks and corresponding Keyframer commands.

TUTORIALS

To do the tutorials, you should have 3D Studio loaded on your screen.

Tutorial 1

In this tutorial you'll create a simple animation with a file that comes with 3D Studio.

1. Go to the Keyframer. Choose *File/Load* and load the file CAFETABL.3DS . This file shows a table and chair .

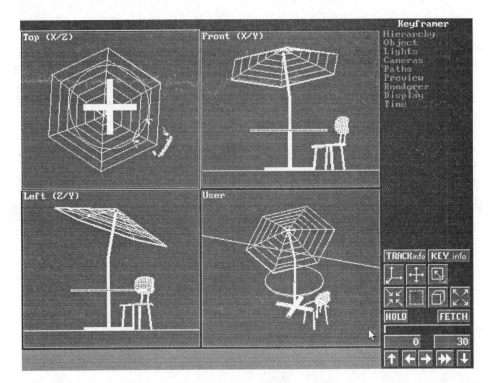

FIGURE 6-17. Mesh file CAFETABL.3DS in Keyframer.

Change the lower right viewport to the camera view. To do this, click on the viewport, then press the C key.

2. Right-click twice on **Zoom Out** to make room to move the camera. Choose the *Cameras* menu option to display the camera.

3. Move the slider at the bottom of the screen to frame 30.

4. Choose *Cameras/Move*. In the Top viewport, move the camera to a new view, such as the one shown below.

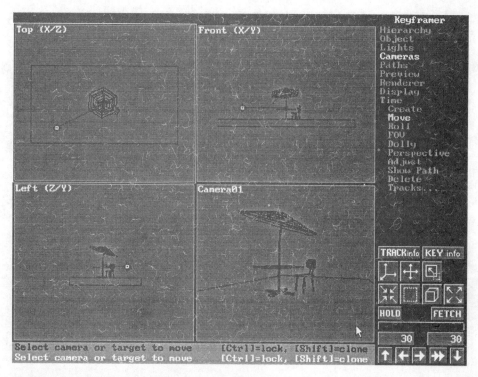

FIGURE 6-18. New camera position for frame 30.

4. Make a preview of the animation. Choose *Preview/Make* and click twice on the camera viewport. When the Make Preview dialog box appears, click on **Preview**. Wait for the preview to be created, then watch the preview.

5. If you like, render the animation by choosing *Renderer/Render* and clicking on the camera view. On the Render Animation dialog box, be sure to click on **Disk** to save the animation file. Enter a filename for your flic. You can later watch the animation with the *Renderer/View/Flic* option.

6. Save the file. Choose *File/Save* and type in the filename CAFETAB2.3DS.

Tutorial 2

In this tutorial you'll add object motion to the scene.

1. Load the file CAFETAB2.3DS from the previous tutorial if it is not already on your screen.

2. Go to frame 30, if you're not there already.

3. Move the chair in the Front viewport. To do this, choose *Object/Move*. Click on the chair in the Front viewport. Move the chair about 90 units upward, as shown below.

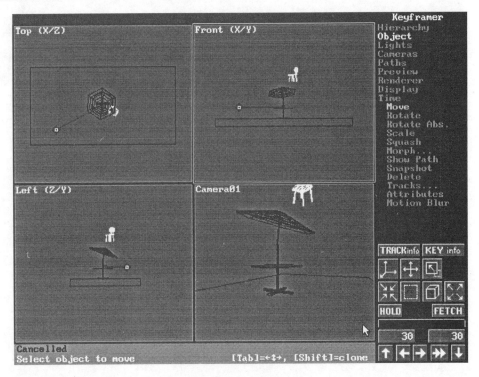

FIGURE 6-19. Chair moved upward on frame 30.

4. Make a preview of the animation. Choose *Preview/Make* and click twice on the camera view. When the Make Preview dialog box appears, click on **Preview**. Wait for the preview to be created, then watch the preview. You can also render the animation if you like.

5. Save the file as CAFETAB3.3DS.

Tutorial 3

In this tutorial you'll use Track Info to make the animation loop seamlessly.

1. Load the file CAFETAB3.3DS from the previous tutorial if it is not already on your screen.

2. Give the animation a total of 60 frames. To do this, click on the total number of frames (30) at the lower right of the screen. Enter **60** and click on **OK**.

3. Right-click on the **Track Info** button. The World track for this model appears.

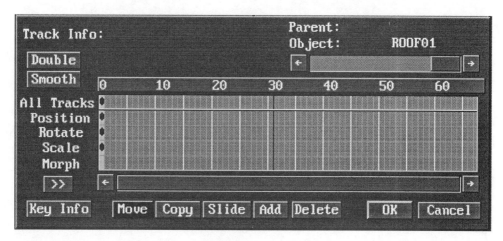

FIGURE 6-20. Track Info screen for World.

4. Copy all tracks on frame 0 to the frame 60. To do this, click on **Copy**, then click under frame **0** next to **All**. Copy the dots to frame **60** and click to set. Click on **OK** to exit Track Info.

The animation will now loop seamlessly.

5. Make a preview of the animation. Choose *Preview/Make* and click on the camera viewport. When the Make Preview dialog box appears, click on **Preview**. Wait for the preview to be created, then watch the preview. You can also render the animation if you like.

6. Save the file as CAFETAB4.3DS.

EXERCISE

Load the model 3DHOUSE.3DS which you made in the last exercise in the previous chapter. If you have not made the file, load the file CAFETABL.3DS.

Create a design plan for a 100-frame animation to be played onscreen.

Go to the Keyframer. Move to each keyframe and move the camera to the appropriate position for the keyframe.

Create a preview of the animation. Adjust the motion if necessary by going to the appropriate keyframes and changing the camera, or by creating new keyframes.

When the preview looks right, render the animation to a flic.

7

VISUALIZATION
TECHNIQUES

Visualization is the art of showing how a design will look when built. So far you've learned how to make a reasonably realistic renderings in 3D Studio. More advanced techniques can be used to increase the degree of realism in your renderings.

MATERIALS

In Chapter 5 you learned how to make basic materials and apply mapping coordinates to objects in your scene. These materials can be improved to increase realism.

A common problem with computer-generated renderings is that everything looks extraordinarily clean, making the image cold and lifeless. In real life, materials such as brick, carpeting and wood have slight variations due to construction, handling and life in general. By adding subtle variations to your materials you can make them look more as if they exist in the real world.

Mapping Assignment

The four rows of buttons and sliders at the bottom of the Materials Editor screen allow you to use bitmaps in a number of ways to increase realism. The most commonly used mapping types are described below.

To choose a bitmap for mapping assignment, click on the word NONE under Maps and directly across from the map type. A file selector appears. Choose the appropriate wildcard type, then choose the bitmap from the list. Move the mapping slider to the desired value. Render the sample sphere to see the effect of the mapping.

Texture. You have already seen how a bitmap can be used as a texture on an object. Sometimes a setting of 100 makes the bitmap too strong, making the rendering look like a cartoon. A strong bitmap can be tempered by lowering the Texture slider and changing the Diffuse color to gray.

When Texture is set to a value lower than 100, the surface gets its color partly from the bitmap and partly from the Diffuse color. If you lower the Texture 1 setting to 75-90 and change the Diffuse color to gray, the bitmap color will be diluted but still clearly visible. This arrangement softens the bitmap and increases the rendering's realism.

Opacity. An opacity map is generally a black and white image. The renderer uses the black and white areas of the applied bitmap to determine areas of the geometry which are opaque, and areas which are transparent. Black pixels cause transparency, white pixels cause opacity. The black and white bitmap image does not appear on the geometry in the rendering, as it would if you used the bitmap as a texture map; the color values of the image are only being used to determine areas of transparency. Where the opacity map is white, the geometry will be rendered using the base colors or texture map you have assigned to the material. Opacity maps can save huge amounts of modeling effort. They can be used to fake holes in objects that would take hours to build from actual geometry. If you ever need to represent a wire mesh or a chain-link fence, you will almost certainly do so with an opacity map.

Bump. A bump map puts dents or bumps in an object without actually changing the geometry. A bump map uses the lightness or darkness of a bitmap to make the bumpiness. For example, the bitmap shown below will produce a surface like the one below.

FIGURE 7-1. Bitmap, and the surface it produces when used as a bump map.

The white portions of the bitmap are raised while the darker portions make indentations.

Every surface has slight bumps in it. An ordinary interior wall, for example, has very small bumps. A bump map applied lightly (1-10) provides a subtle variation to a material. Adding a bump map to your material may dramatically increase your rendering time, so use a bump map only when necessary.

Reflection. A reflection map makes a material look as if it's reflecting a bitmap. When you set up a reflection map, 3D Studio makes a giant imaginary sphere around the scene and maps the bitmap to the sphere. 3D Studio then figures out what parts of the bitmap will reflect on the object based on the current scene setup.

A reflection map is useful for giving an object the appearance of existing in the real world. All objects in life reflect the scene around them to a greater or lesser degree. A reflection map, lightly applied to shiny objects, adds realism to a rendering.

For highly reflective objects such as windows, set the Reflection slider to a high value such as 80. For a subtle reflection, set the slider between 5 and 15.

Bitmaps

3D Studio comes with many bitmaps. Three of these are especially useful for making subtle changes to materials.

To see any of these bitmaps in the Materials Editor, choose *Options/View Image File.* A file selector appears. Click on the appropriate wildcard selector, then choose the file. After a few moments the file appears on the screen. Press **ESC** to return to the Materials Editor.

CEMENT.CEL. This bitmap is made up of black, white and gray dots. It is useful for adding subtle variations with nearly every mapping type. When used as a bump map it adds small, even bumps across a surface.

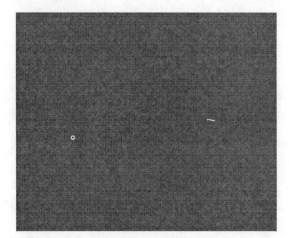

FIGURE 7-2. Bitmap CEMENT.CEL.

REFMAP.GIF. This bitmap consists of black, gray and white smudges.

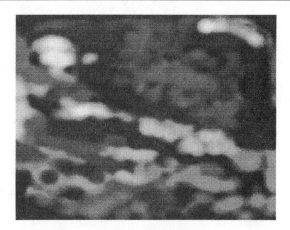

FIGURE 7-3 Bitmap REFMAP.GIF.

REFMAP.GIF is useful as a reflection map for lending a "chrome" look to curved surfaces.

VALLEY_L.TGA. This bitmap is a scanned photograph of an outdoor scene. Because of its many and varied colors, VALLEY_L.TGA makes an excellent reflection map for shiny objects such as glass.

FIGURE 7-4. Bitmap VALLEY_L.TGA

Variations Summary

If your renderings look too clean and cold, try warming them up by varying your materials. The following is a guide to mapping variations for architectural renderings.

Texture 1   Lower to 75-90
Diffuse color   Change to medium gray
Bump   CEMENT.CEL at 1-10
Reflection   VALLEY_L.TGA or REFMAP.GIF at 5-15

You can, of course, use any bitmaps you like for mapping assignment. The settings above have been found to work well for architectural renderings.

Subtle changes to materials are often not clearly visible on the sample sphere in the Materials Editor. In addition, these changes are often difficult to detect in the rendering itself. The rendering just looks better, although the viewer will find it hard to say exactly why.

For further information on mapping assignment, see the *3D Studio Reference Manual.*

Self Illumination

Self illumination makes an object look as if it's lit up. This technique is useful for making lamp globes, car headlights and streetlights.

LIGHTING

One of the most important elements of a good scene is its lighting. In this section, you'll learn how to set up realistic lighting.

Bouncing Light

A spotlight alone casts a "harsh" light which only illuminates a specific area, leaving the rest of the model very dark. Omni lights fill in the dark areas, making a more realistic rendering.

Figure 7-5 shows two renderings of a house. In the first rendering, just one shadow-casting spotlight illuminates the scene. In the second, three omni lights have been added to the scene.

FIGURE 7-5. Two exterior renderings.

In real life, light bounces off objects to illuminate hidden areas. For example, look under the table you're sitting at right now. Although no light shines directly onto the floor under the table, it is still somewhat illuminated to the point where you can see the floor quite clearly. This effect is called *radiosity.*

3D Studio does not account for radiosity; light rays shine in a straight line and do not bounce. For this reason you must place dim lights in your scene to simulate "bounced" light. Because omni lights shine through objects they are excellent for simulating bounced light.

See the two renderings below. In the first rendering, the only light is a shadow-casting spotlight above the table. The shadow is unrealistically dark. In the second rendering a dim omni light was placed near the floor under the table. Because bouncing light is taken into account, the second rendering is more realistic.

FIGURE 7-6. Two interior renderings.

Lighting Setups

A workable lighting setup consists of two or more omni lights augmented by a shadow-casting spotlight. Figure 7-6 shows a typical lighting setup for an outdoor architectural rendering.

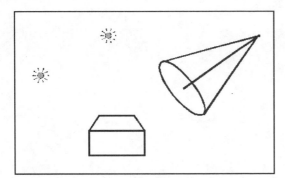

FIGURE 7-7. Standard exterior lighting setup.

An omni light can also be placed below the house to illuminate the underside of the eaves, if they will be visible in the scene.

For an interior rendering, a similar approach can be used. In the setup below, a shadow-casting spotlight has been placed at the top of the vase, while an omni light below fills in the dark areas.

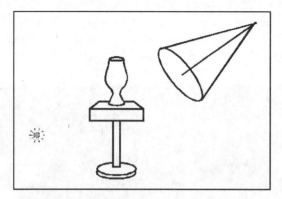

FIGURE 7-8. Standard interior lighting setup.

SHADOWS

In order to have shadows in a rendering, you must have a spotlight, an object to cast a shadow, and an object upon which the shadow will fall.

Each component of the shadow scene must be set up for the shadow, as follows:

Spotlight. Place a spotlight in the scene. Make sure the spotlight's cone falls around the object to cast a shadow. To check the cone, choose *Lights/Spot/Adjust* and turn on **Show Cone**. The spotlight cone appears on the screen, showing you the spotlight's scope.

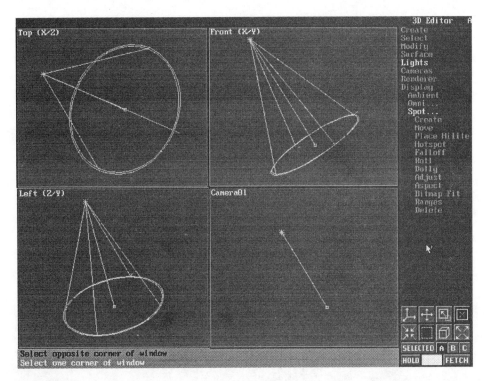

FIGURE 7-9. Spotlight cone.

The spotlight must also have its **Shadow** attribute turned on. To turn on this attribute, choose *Lights/Spot/Adjust* and click on the spotlight. The Spotlight dialog box appears.

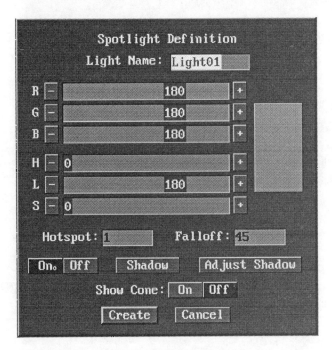

FIGURE 7-10. Spotlight Definition dialog box.

Click on the **Casts Shadows** button to turn it on.

Object Casting Shadow. The object casting the shadow must have its **Casts Shadows** attribute turned on. By default this attribute is automatically turned on when an object is created or imported in a DXF file. To check that this attribute is turned on, choose *Modify/Object/Attributes* and click on the object. The Object Attributes dialog box appears.

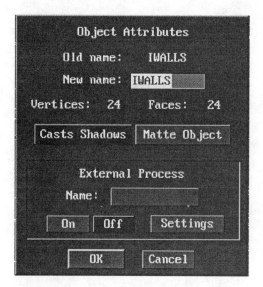

FIGURE 7-11. Object Attributes dialog box.

Check to make sure the **Casts Shadows** button is on.

Rendering. Both the Render Still Image and Render Animation dialog boxes contain a **Shadows** option. When you render, the **Shadows** button must be turned on in order to see shadows in your rendering. This button is turned on by default.

Troubleshooting

If you set up a scene with shadows and none appear in the scene, check the all the settings mentioned above. If the shadows still don't appear, check the following.

Spotlight angle. If the spotlight is too low in relationship to the object casting the shadow, a shadow will not appear in the scene.

To understand this concept, consider a vase sitting on a table. If you draw a line from the spotlight to the vase, then from the vase to the table, the line forms an angle. If the angle is too close to 90 degrees, the shadow will not render.

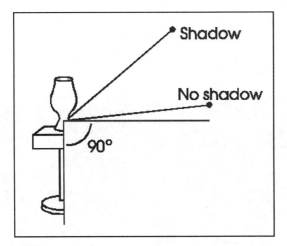

FIGURE 7-12. Spotlight angle for shadows cannot be close to 90 degrees.

In the example on the left the shadow will not appear. To make the shadow appear, move the spotlight upward as shown in the example on the right.

Other lights too bright. In any scene with shadows it's a good idea to put in a few omni lights. These lights will fill in the dark areas of the scene as well as keep the shadows from being too harsh.

If your omni lights are too bright in comparison to the shadow-casting spotlight, they will wash out the shadows. To check for this problem, try turning off all the omni lights to see if the shadows appear. To turn off an omni light choose *Lights/Omni/Adjust*, click on the omni light and click the **Off** button. The omni light will turn black on the screen, indicating that it is off.

Render the scene again. If the shadow appears, this means the omni lights were too bright. Try cutting each omni light's Luminance value in half.

Self-Illumination. If the object receiving the shadow holds a self-illuminated material, then it will not show shadows. If you want to see a shadow on the object, eliminate its material's self-illumination in the Materials Editor.

TUTORIALS

Tutorial 1

1. Load 3D Studio if necesssary. Make sure you're in the 3D Editor by checking the module name at the upper right of the screen. Load the file 3DHOUSE.3DS from *Tutorial 1, Chapter 5*.

2. Place an additional camera inside the house as shown. Use *Cameras/Create* to create the camera. To change the camera view to the new camera, click on the Camera01 viewport and press the **C** key. Choose Camera02 from the list. Use *Cameras/Move* to move the camera to the position shown below.

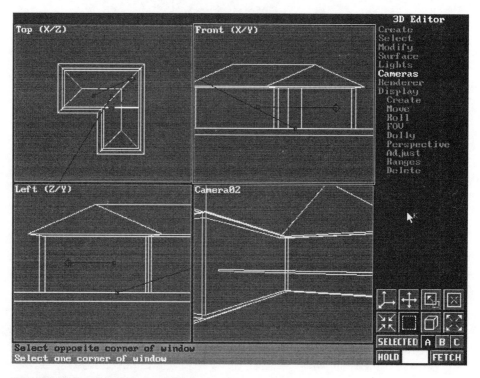

FIGURE 7-13. Camera placement.

3. Next you'll import a chair from the file CAFETABL.3DS. First, select all the objects in this scene. To do this, choose *File/Merge*. The following dialog box appears:

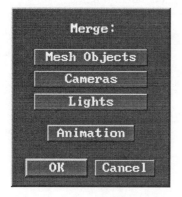

Turn off all options except **Mesh Objects** and click on **OK**.

A file selector appears. Select the file CAFETABL.3DS. A list of objects in the file appears. Click on the object name **chairscafe**. Click on **OK** to import the chair object.

The object is very small. In order to see it, choose *Select/Object/By Name*. Select the object **chairscafe**. The chair will turn red on the screen.

To make the chair a more appropriate size it must be scaled. To do this, first turn on the local axis. Next, choose *Modify/Object/3D Scale*. Click on the chair. Scale it up to 400% twice, then scale it to 190%.

The chair is now the right size but is in the wrong place. Choose *Modify/Object/Move*. Move the chair in the Top, Front and Left viewports until it sits in the scene, as shown below.

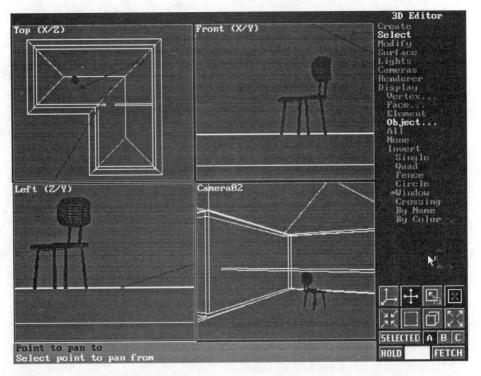

FIGURE 7-14. Chair placement.

4. Assign the material BLUE FABRIC to the floor. To do this, choose *Surface/Material/Choose* and select the material BLUE FABRIC from the list. Choose *Surface/Material/Assign/By Name* and select the object FLOOR01. Click on **OK**, then click on **OK** again to confirm assignment of the material to the tagged object.

5. Create and assign mapping coordinates to the floor. To do this, zoom in on the floor in the Top viewport. Choose *Surface/Mapping/Adjust/Scale* and scale the mapping icon until it's a little bigger than the chair. Choose *Surface/Mapping/ Apply/Object* and press the **H** key. Choose the object FLOOR01 from the list to assign the mapping coordinates to the floor.

6. Render the camera view.

7. Save the file as 3DHOUSE2.3DS.

Tutorial 2

1. Load the file 3DHOUSE2.3DS from the previous tutorial.

2. Create a spotlight in the scene. Choose *Lights/Spot/Create* and place the spotlight in the Top viewport with a Luminance of 220. Turn the **Show Cone** button on.

Move the spotlight with the *Lights/Spot/Move* command to position it as shown.

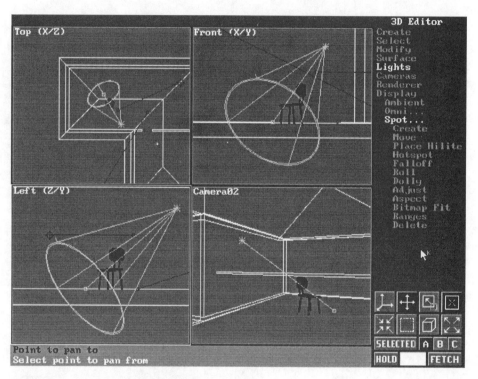

FIGURE 7-15. Spotlight placement.

3. Make sure the spotlight is set up to cast shadows. Choose *Lights/Spot/Adjust* and click on the spotlight. Turn the **Shadow** attribute on.

4. Right-click on **Zoom Extents**. Turn off the omni light at the lower right corner of the Top viewport. Choose *Lights/Omni/Adjust* and click on the omni light. Click on the **Off** button under the color sliders to turn the light off. The light should now appear black on the screen rather than yellow.

5. Render the camera view. The chair should cast a shadow on the floor in the scene. If it doesn't, read over the Shadows section of this chapter. Check each item required to make shadows appear.

6. Save the file as 3DHOUSE3.3DS.

EXERCISE

Experiment with the materials in 3DHOUSE3.3DS. To do this, load the file and go to the Materials Editor. Choose *Materials/Get from Scene* and pick a material from the scene. The material is rendered on the sample sphere in one of the boxes.

To change the material, add a bump map such as CEMENT.CEL, or add a reflection map such as VALLEY_L.TGA. Reduce or increase Shininess and Shininess Strength, or change the Diffuse color. Render the sample sphere to get an idea of how the changed material will look.

When you are satisfied with your changes to a material, choose Material/Put to Scene and put the changed material to the scene. You can then click on the next sample box, pull in another material and make more changes.

When you have finished making changes to the scene, to the 3D Editor and render the scene again. Repeat until you are satisfied with the results.

-Notes-

-Notes-

-Notes-

-Notes-

-Notes-

-Notes-

-Notes-

-Notes-

-Notes-

-Notes-

-Notes-